WORLD'S GREATEST WONDERS

A FAMILY REFERENCE GUIDE

WORLD'S GREATEST WONDERS

FROM MAN-MADE MASTERPIECES TO BREATHTAKING SUPRISES OF NATURE

Parragon

Bath • New York • Singapore • Hong Kong • Cologne • Delhi
Melbourne • Amsterdam • Johannesburg • Shenzhen

First published by Parragon in 2013

Parragon
Chartist House
15–17 Trim Street
Bath, BA1 1HA, UK
www.parragon.com

ISBN 978-1-4723-2050-6
Printed in China

CONTENTS

Introduction

We live on a unique planet. The only one so far discovered that has life, as well as great geological and biological diversity. These two factors have provided an extraordinary place to live. The action of the natural forces which have sculpted the earth's surface for millions of years has been supplemented by the great creative spirit of human beings, who have built their own wonders since the beginning of civilisation. We have before us a whole world, our own to explore and discover, to find and revel in the natural paradises created by the patient hand of nature as well as the astonishing constructions imagined by the genius of humankind. You just have to look around and take in the spectacle.

MAN-MADE WONDERS

The creative impulse of human beings

If there is one thing that distinguishes human beings from the other creatures that inhabit the Earth, it is their creative ability. Since the beginnings of civilisation, men and women have imagined and carried out imposing constructions, defying the laws of nature. From the Egyptian pyramids at Giza to the Sydney Opera House, from the Taj Mahal to the Terracotta Army of Xian, these works show us the ingenuity to resolve technical challenges and the capacity to create works of great beauty which have driven civilisation through the centuries in every corner of our planet.

STONEHENGE

Stonehenge An enigmatic aura surrounds the construction and the use of this megalithic complex located 120 km (75 mi) west of London.

The mystery of the stones

For centuries, many explanatory theories have been debated about the rings of menhirs found at Stonehenge. However, its mystery and the fascination it generates have transcended time and still enthral to this day.

A construction, whose origins are buried deep in an unknown history, is an invitation to explore the mysterious. Around 120 km (75 mi) west of London, on the plains outside Salisbury, on an open embankment measuring almost 100 m (328 ft) in diameter, one of these enigmatic constructions stands tall: Stonehenge. This megalithic monument built over two millennia, almost 5,000 years ago, has opened the windows to our imagination. Some of our ideas and fantasies have grown alongside scientific research, and studies that have attempted to reveal how and why enormous menhirs weighing up to 25 tonnes were buried in a circle, in line with the passage of the Sun and the Moon, by a Neolithic civilisation about which virtually nothing is known.

Merlin, druids and petrified giants

During the first half of the 12th century, Welsh cleric Geoffrey of Monmouth made public in his writings a popular legend: the stones at Stonehenge were petrified giants and the circles they formed were known as the Giants' Dance. The priest, passionate for the legend of King Arthur, wrote *The Prophecy of Merlin* and *The Life of Merlin* between 1135 and 1154. He attributed the menhirs to the wizard, who he stated brought the stones from Ireland with the help of a group of Breton knights. He even wrote that they served as a memorial to Uther Pendragon and the father of King Arthur. This was the first written reference to Stonehenge.

Today, it is known that the technique of dragging used by primitive civilisations, prior to the Copper Age, was an intelligent and efficient means of building such a construction, dismissing the notion that magical fantasy was responsible for their presence. However, for the majority of the medieval period, the legend promoted was that the monument had been created by the druids, the priests of Celtic tribes, as a temple that served a ritual purpose and to call the Gods of nature. This belief was further embedded, during the 17th century, when British historian and author John Aubrey wrote his theory that linked the origins of Stonehenge to this group of pagan priests. At the beginning of the 18th century, this view

↑Circles The Stonehenge complex is structured in four concentric rings of different-sized menhirs and trilithons.

was further upheld by English doctor and archaeologist William Stukeley, a druid fanatic who was influenced by his status as a Freemason. Stukeley's views had consequences. The Ancient Order of the Druids, a London-based Freemason group created in 1833, brought its members together at Stonehenge every summer solstice to perform presumably druid rituals, until 1985, when the British Government passed legislation protecting and preserving the monument, thereby prohibiting the performance of such acts.

However, in the 17th century, other versions of the mystery were put forward. The Roman and Anglican churches viewed the megalithic monuments with suspicion, claiming they were temples suspected of feeding witchcraft and devil worship. As a result, farmers from neighbouring towns used stones from Stonehenge as building material when erecting houses, with popular sentiment contributing to the destruction of the cursed construction. The theory of prestigious architect Inigo Jones was less destructive; in 1620, and on the orders of James I of England and VI of Scotland, he investigated the circular formations with his team of experts, leading to the conclusion that it was a Roman temple, dedicated to Caelus (equivalent to the Greek god Uranus) built in 79 BC.

The research of Sir Norman Lockyer at the beginning of the 20th century served to link the mysterious formations with astronomical observation and a place where ancient civilisations worshipped the Sun and the Moon. His first calculations dated completion of the construction at around 1800 BC, thus dismissing the theory that they had been erected by Celtic Druids, who populated southern England from 300 BC. It also served to dismiss Jones' Roman Temple theory, as the Romans did not reach the British Isles until around 55 BC, led by Julius Caesar.

↖**Moat** The monument is encompassed by a circular moat measuring 104 m (341 ft) in diameter.

↑**The remains** Of the dozens of monoliths, only a few remain standing. However, they serve to provide an idea of how the complex originally looked.

←**Immense** The largest monoliths weigh up to 25 tonnes each.

↑**Trilithons** The inner circle is made up of trilithons: two menhirs crowned by a horizontal flagstone.

Archaeological and technological advances in the last century have helped to further refine knowledge about the site. Thus, it is understood that Stonehenge was built in three phases. The first started around 3100 BC; this involved the excavation of 56 holes that surround the formation, known as Aubrey holes, and the introduction of the stones called 'the four seasons'. The second phase started one thousand years afterwards, when 80 blocks of bluestone were placed in a semicircle. This type of stone was found in the Preseli Hills, in South West Wales, 320 km (199 mi) from Stonehenge. It is speculated that they were transported on rafts from the Welsh coast to Bristol, then upriver on the Avon. It is believed that they were then transported over land on rollers created from tree trunks. Other siliceous rocks were transported from Marlborough Hills, around 30 km (19 mi) north of where the monument is located. The third phase began in around 1500 BC, when it is understood that the trilithons and the Altar stone were set in place. It is believed that the site was abandoned 400 years later. Was it a place of worship, or perhaps an astronomical observatory? The mystery goes on.

A perfect circle

Stonehenge was constructed in several phases; however, it is believed that it took its final shape in around 1500 BC.

Lintel The horizontal slabs weigh 7 tonnes. It is supposed they were elevated using towers of tree trunks.

The Sun On the summer solstice, the sun crosses the axis of the construction. As a result, it is commonly believed that the builders of the complex had an understanding of astronomy.

Second ring Formed by smaller blocks of bluestone than those of the outer circle.

THE STRUCTURE

Stonehenge is formed of concentric circles of megaliths up to 5 m (16 ft) high. It is perfectly arranged on the ground to calculate the journey of the Sun and the Moon and predict solstices and eclipses.

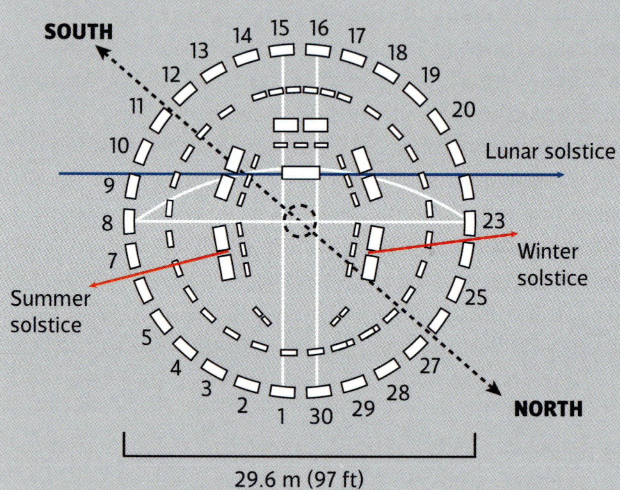

The altar At the centre, a slab of micaceous sandstone can be found.
Fourth ring Comprising a cromlech, a horseshoe-shaped structure made up of 19 menhirs measuring 3 m (10 ft) in height.
First ring Measuring 30 m (98 ft) in diameter and comprising 30 sandstone monoliths weighing 25 tonnes each, united by a continuous lintel. Today, only seven remain standing.
Third ring An assembly of five trilithons arranged in the shape of a horseshoe. Each one is formed by two menhirs crowned by a 4.4 m (14.4 ft) lintel.

PYRAMIDS OF GIZA

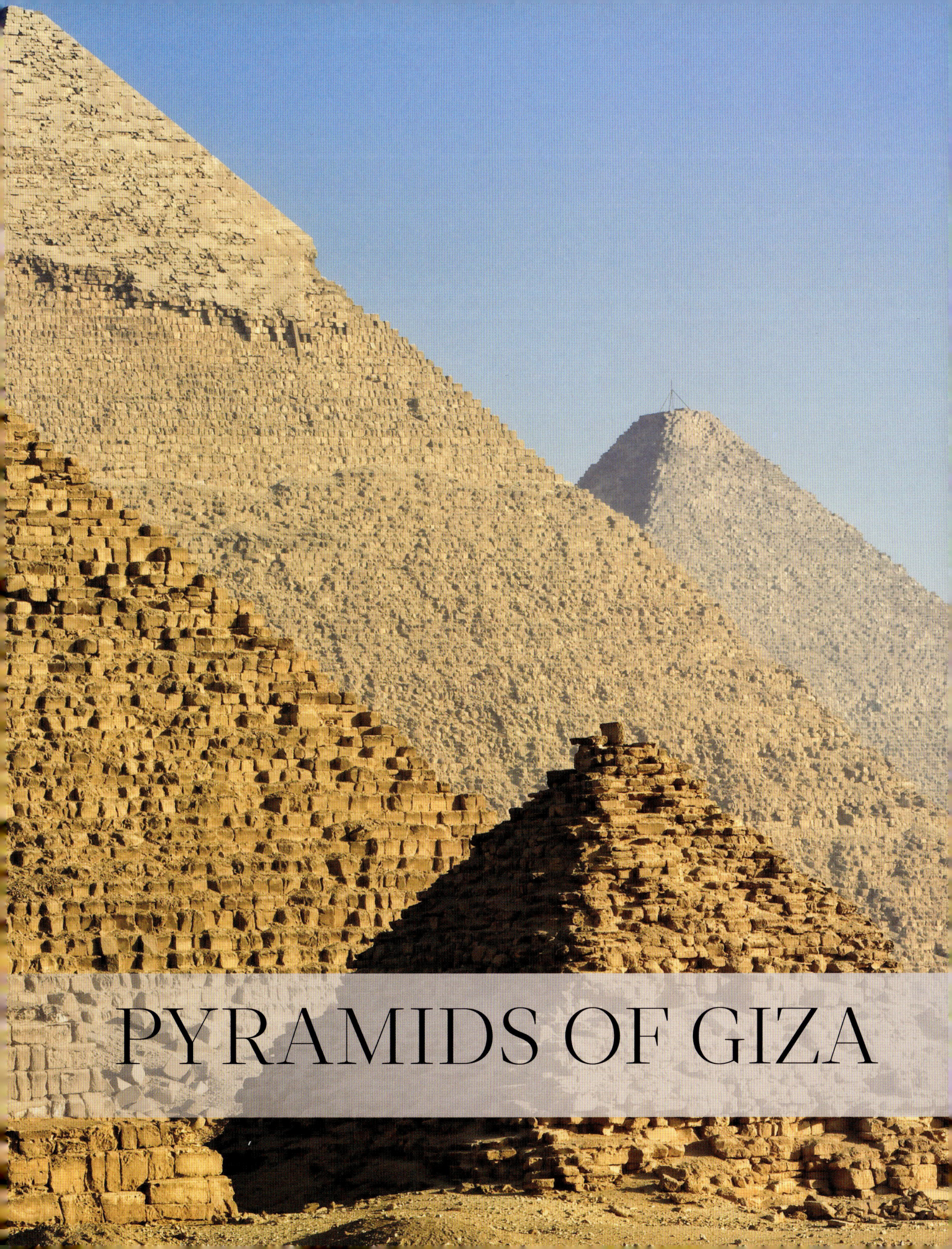

Giza The Giza necropolis, where the three pyramids are located, is around 20 km (12 mi) south of Cairo, the Egyptian capital.

A tribute to a former era

At the Ancient Egyptian necropolis in Giza, the pyramids of Khufu, Khafra and Menkaure, together with the Sphinx, form part of one of the world's most spectacular mortuary complexes.

The three pyramids at Giza are the oldest of the Ancient Wonders of the World and the only ones to have survived to this day. Built over 4,600 years ago, their sheer size and the ingenuity required to build them continue to surprise. The way they are photographed makes it appear as if they are located deep in the barren desert. In fact, they are located within the metropolitan area of Cairo, at about 10 km (6 mi) from the city centre and very close to where the capital of the Ancient Egyptian Empire, Memphis, once stood.

'Khufu's Horizon' (the largest pyramid), 'Khafra is Great' and 'Menkaure is Divine' were the names given to these monuments when translated into Ancient Greek. One curious fact is that at no time does the word 'pyramid' appear, as it did not exist in hieroglyphics. They were built during the second half of the third millennium BC under the orders of three kings of the 4th dynasty of the Ancient Egyptian Empire: Khufu, Khafra and Menkaure. At the time, the Giza Plains formed part of a large area of more than 25 mi of the Lower Nile where important, populous cities to the South of Memphis once stood. Over this strip of land, from North to South, there were three large cemeteries: Giza, Sakkara and Dashur. Each of these cemeteries had enormous monuments and smaller tombs.

Despite the significant amount of information recovered on Ancient Egypt, only a little more than 20 per cent of these archaeological complexes and other smaller cemeteries in the area have been excavated, such as Abusir, Abu Gorab and Zawyet el-Aryan which continue to hide much of the knowledge of the ancient civilisation. Sakkara is the oldest necropolis, and was designed around 2700 BC by Imhotep, considered the father of mortuary architecture and adored as a demigod.

However, Giza is the most spectacular complex; it is here that the most impressive works can be found. The Great Pyramid, which attracts the most attention, originally measured more than 230 m (755 ft) in width and almost 147 m (482 ft) in height; however, due to erosion over the

↑Alignment Certain theories debate the fact that the three pyramids are aligned with the planets (Saturn, Venus and Mercury) or with Orion's Belt.

centuries, its height has been reduced to 137 m (449 ft). It is estimated that when construction was completed, in around 2570 BC, it would have weighed around six million tonnes. As part of the pyramid's construction, around 3.2 million blocks of stone were used, a figure that impressed Napoleon Bonaparte during the conquest of Egypt at the beginning of the 19th century. According to the French Emperor, the limestone rocks used to build the Great Pyramid would have been sufficient to build a wall of 3 m (10 ft) around the entire perimeter of France.

The uniqueness of the construction lies in the fact that of the three burial chambers, two were located within the pyramid with a third one beneath ground level, connected by an intricate network of narrow tunnels, the purpose of which remains unclear. One of the higher chambers was to be used by Khufu, but in general, in the majority of the monumental tombs, the burial chambers were underground. According to Greek historian Herodotus, 100,000 men were needed over a thirty-year period to build the pyramid. In truth, the first ten years were used to build the work ramp, and work on the construction itself only took place during the three months in which the Nile was at its highest, when workers could not work the fields.

Millennial splendour

The pyramid dedicated to the Pharaoh Khafra (2558–2532 BC), the second largest, although it appears a little higher as it is located on a small hill, measures one metre less than Khufu's pyramid. It is also somewhat smaller in width, measuring around 215 m (705 ft) in diameter. Whereas the third largest pyramid, dedicated to Menkaure (2514–2486 BC), does not even hold one's attention when compared to the others, despite measuring 108 m (354 ft) in width and approximately 66 m (217 ft) in height.

↑The Sphinx Image of the Great Sphinx of Giza, located in front of the pyramids.

↗Exposed stone There is little evidence of the original smooth limestone finishes.

↗The Great Gallery This passage in the pyramid of Khufu rises 47 m (154 ft) to the burial chamber.

→Esplanade Aerial view of the Giza esplanade with the three pyramids.

↑Reliefs Close-up of one of the reliefs at the Giza complex.

Around the complex of three pyramids, there are hundreds of 'mastabas', tombs built in 'streets' and also private burial chambers, located some distance away, in the quarries that surround the complex. However, the structure that most attracts one's attention, the three pyramids aside, is the Sphinx; an immense structure with the body of a lion and, supposedly, the face of Khafra, which stands in front of the entrance to this great pharaoh's pyramid. The Sphinx was sculpted on an immense 57 m (187 ft) long, 20 m (66 ft) high rock. And although the rock only has one colour today due to erosion, during the first centuries after its creation, its exterior contained different colours: the head and body were red, whilst the nemes that covered its head was decorated with blue and yellow stripes. The residents of Giza called it Abu el-Hol (father of terror), given the penetrating look in its eyes. The monument has deteriorated over time: neither its nose, all broken as a result of armed conflict, nor its artificial beard, which came off and can now be seen in the British Museum, have been preserved. More recently, part of its right shoulder has also collapsed.

The Great Pyramid of Giza

The pyramid of the Pharaoh Khufu or Cheops is the largest at the Giza necropolis that also houses temples, cemeteries and other, smaller pyramids.

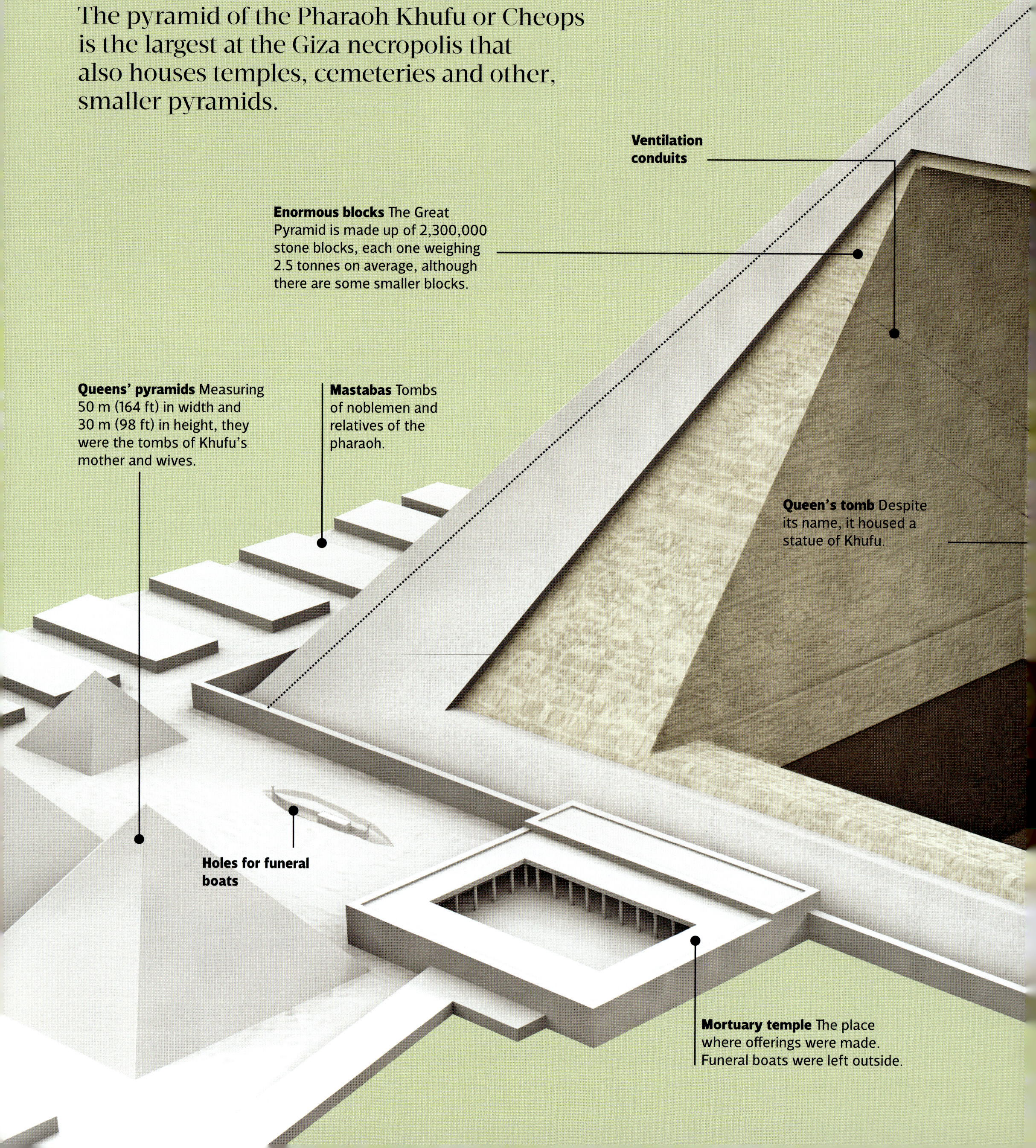

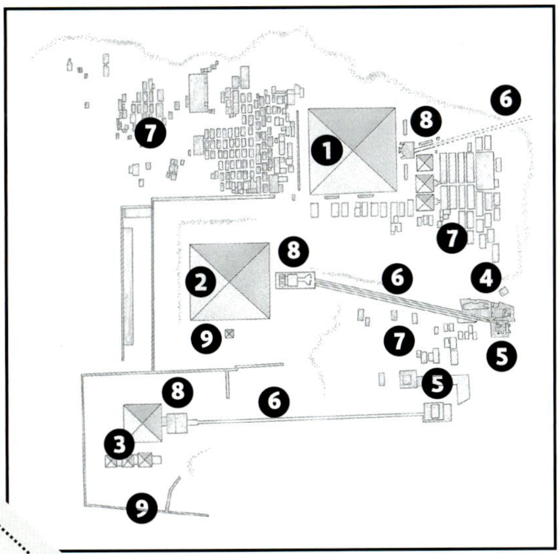

The Giza plateau houses the three most famous Egyptian pyramids: the pyramids of Khufu and his son Khafra and the pyramid of Menkaure. Each one contains a complex in which the same elements are repeated, with the exception of the Sphinx which belongs to the pyramid of Khafra.

1. Khufu
2. Khafra
3. Menkaure
4. Great Sphinx
5. Great Temple
6. Procession route
7. Dignitary's mastaba
8. Mortuary temple
9. Secondary pyramid

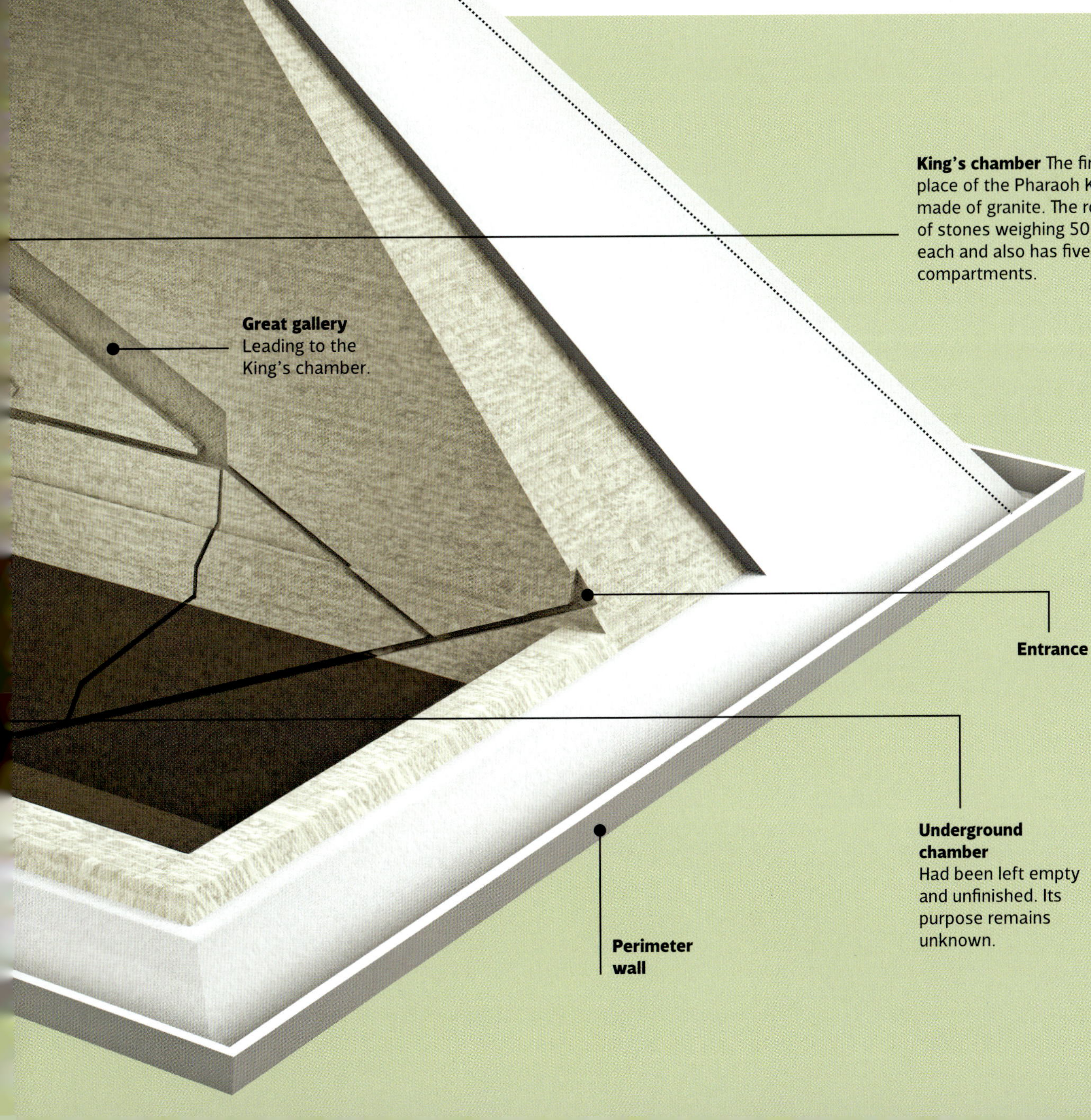

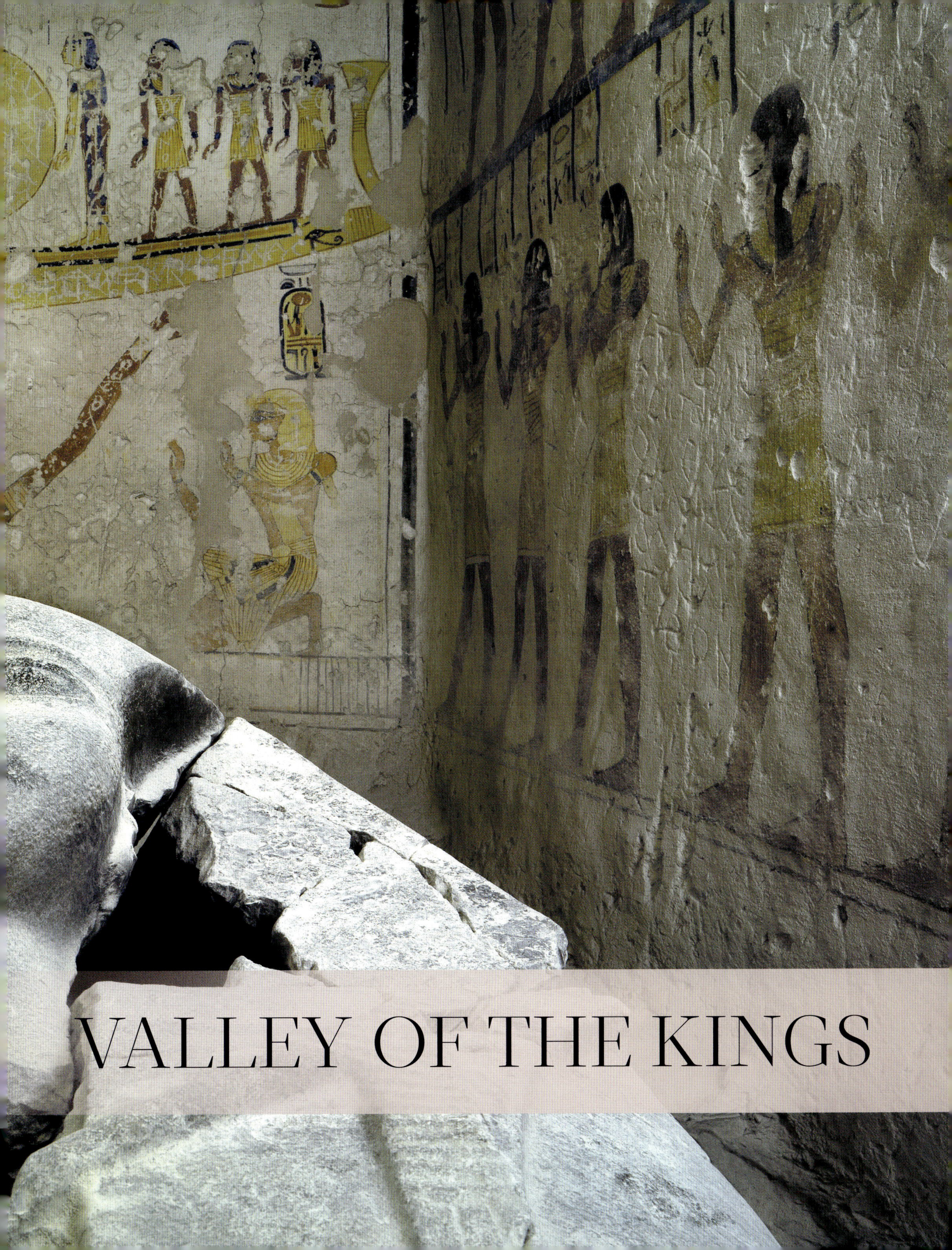

VALLEY OF THE KINGS

Valley of the Kings This mortuary complex is located close to Luxor, 600 km (373 mi) to the south of Cairo following the course of the River Nile.

The burial ground of the Pharaohs

The 63 tombs discovered to date at the Valley of the Kings necropolis are the ultimate testament to the Pharaohs that governed Egypt during the New Kingdom.

Tutankhamen is the key name. Following the discovery of this young Pharaoh's tomb by Howard Carter in 1922, the necropolis in which it was found, the Valley of the Kings, gained a reputation and became the focus of attention for archaeologists and historians of Ancient Egypt. Currently, this area of desert located 600 km (373 mi) to the south of Cairo, on the western banks of the Nile, comprises 63 tombs, half of which belong to Pharaohs of the New Kingdom who chose the spot as their royal cemetery.

This location is no coincidence. Opposite, on the other side of the Nile, was Thebes, the glorious capital of the New Kingdom. At the time, this city replaced the former power centre of Memphis, the capital of the Old Kingdom and home to the monumental pyramids. Unlike their predecessors, the Pharaohs who governed between 1570 and 1085 BC preferred to distance their tombs from mortuary temples, to reduce the risk of looting. Today, those grand temples dedicated to each Pharaoh can be seen on the green and urbanised banks of the river.

The Valley of the Kings itself, where the Pharaohs were buried, is located around 5 km (3 mi) to the west of the river, in a rocky, desert area.

Underground treasure

The apparently mundane reed-covered surface hides a truly exciting secret underground. The layer of rock conceals the wealth of the tombs of Pharaohs and noblemen, with the kings of the New Kingdom having exchanged the magnificence of the pyramids, where their ancestors were buried, for the silent and hidden luxury of an underground burial site. The layout of each tomb is very similar: a large entryway that leads to a shaft, an antechamber with columns, and a room with pillars, or the royal chamber, in which the Pharaoh's sarcophagus was laid to rest.

The necropolis is divided into two areas: the eastern valley and the western valley. On the western valley there are only four tombs, belonging to Amenhotep III (1390–1352 BC) and Ay (1327–1323 BC), Tutankhamen's

↑Seti I One of the rich mural paintings that adorns the tomb of Seti I.

↗Tutankhamen Close-up of the Pharaoh's mortuary mask, made using gold and lapis lazuli stone.

↗Underground View of the central area of the valley with entrances to the tombs of Tutankhamen at the centre, and Ramesses II to the left.

successor, with a further two that have remained unidentified. On the eastern valley, however, there are 59 tombs in total. The oldest belongs to Thutmose I, who governed between 1525 and 1512 BC, which was discovered in 1899. The final Pharaoh to be buried at the necropolis was Ramesses XI, the last king of the 20th dynasty, who governed between 1099 and 1069 BC. According to archaeologists, the best designed tomb belonged to Seti I. Here, following its discovery in 1817, the Litany of Re was discovered. This funerary text, reserved for nobility, invoked the sun god as a reference to the deceased. From Ramesses IV (1153–1147 BC) onwards, the roofs of the tombs were decorated with imagery from the Book of the Dead, which reproduced the legend of the relationship between the Sun and the heavenly bodies.

The discovery of the tomb of Tutankhamen, one of the three that was not looted in the valley, was a turning point as it facilitated access to the four rooms in the gallery, found as they had been originally left after the entrance to the tomb was sealed. There were also ornaments, objects, garments, the sarcophagus containing his body and his treasure, all in their original glory. It was a unique discovery. However, 83 years after Carter's discovery, in 2005, just when it had been accepted that there were no further burials to be discovered, a group of archaeologists entered a previously untouched gallery containing seven sealed sarcophagi. The tomb was called KV63 (the initials

↑Ramesses V Passageway that leads to the burial chamber of Ramesses V.

→Colossi of Memnon These statues preside over the entrance to the mortuary complex of the Pharaoh Amenhotep III, located in Thebes.

↑Artwork Bas-reliefs with Egyptian hieroglyphics at the tomb of Ramesses III.

↗Amenhotep II Inside the burial chamber, the sarcophagus of Amenhotep III.

are an abbreviation for the Valley of the Kings and the number corresponds to the order in which the tombs were discovered).

Techniques for preserving bodies

In the tomb, they found materials used to preserve bodies, dozens of garlands of interwoven flowers, and other religious artefacts. Covered in resin moulds that displayed the face of their occupants, the sarcophagi were, however, empty. Further investigation, not only provided information on the natural substances used during the embalming process and tissue treatment, but also raised suspicion that perhaps the mother of Tutankhamen had been buried in the tomb. This is one of the mysteries that has remained unsolved at the ancient necropolis, in addition to another one that continues to defy scientists: KV5, a tomb from which debris is still being removed, may be the largest of the entire valley. The most recent research has indicated that many of the 150 children that Ramesses II is believed to have fathered are buried in the tomb.

The tomb of Tutankhamen

The tomb of this young Pharaoh was the greatest archaeological discovery at the Valley of the Kings necropolis.

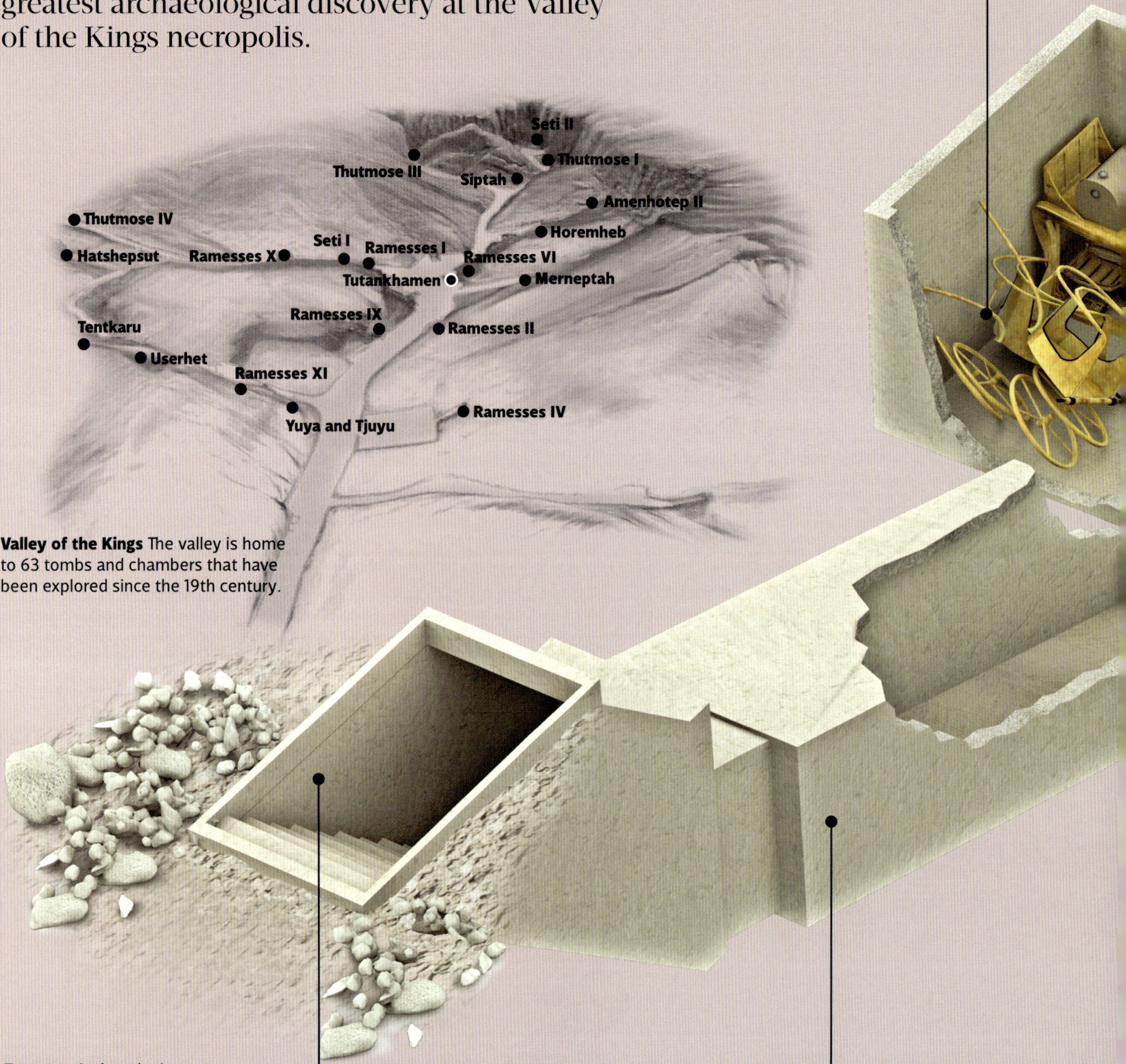

Valley of the Kings The valley is home to 63 tombs and chambers that have been explored since the 19th century.

Antechamber This room was full of valuable carved objects made from gold and gilded wood that belonged to the Pharaoh.

Entrance Archaeologist Howard Carter discovered this entrance on 24 November 1922. It was hidden on the valley's rocky floor.

Access The passage that leads to the tomb measures 1.7 m (5.6 ft) in width and 2 m (6.6 ft) in height.

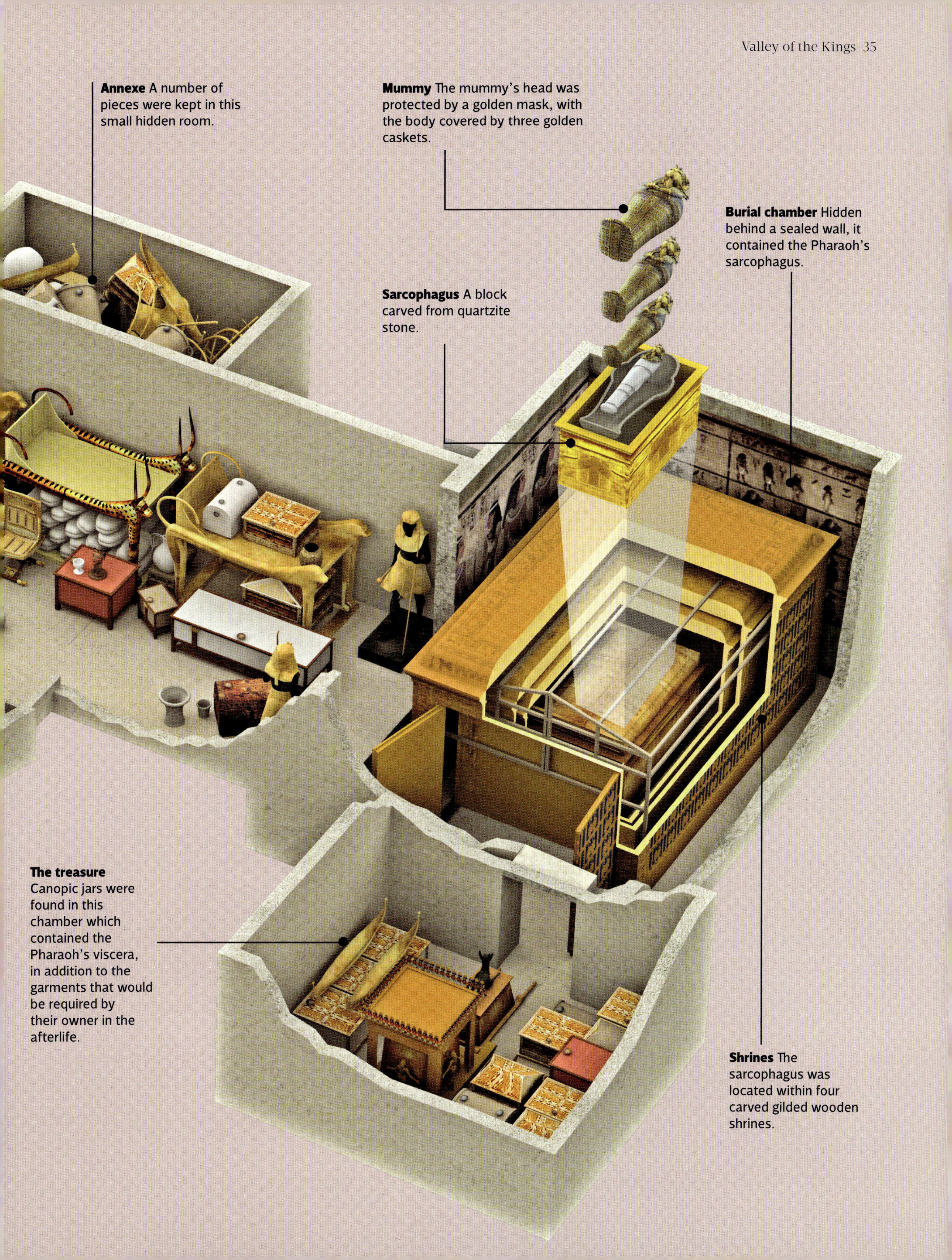
Annexe A number of pieces were kept in this small hidden room.
Mummy The mummy's head was protected by a golden mask, with the body covered by three golden caskets.
Burial chamber Hidden behind a sealed wall, it contained the Pharaoh's sarcophagus.
Sarcophagus A block carved from quartzite stone.
The treasure Canopic jars were found in this chamber which contained the Pharaoh's viscera, in addition to the garments that would be required by their owner in the afterlife.
Shrines The sarcophagus was located within four carved gilded wooden shrines.

PETRA

Petra The ancient city of the Nabataeans is located in the valley of Arava, which runs from the Dead Sea to the Gulf of Aqaba.

A sculpted city

Petra, surrounded by desert mountains, with its buildings cut into the rock, is a unique marvel that has survived in the heart of Jordan for more than 24 centuries.

In the 3rd century BC, the merchant caravans crossed the Middle East with hundreds of camels, from the Persian Gulf to Egypt and from Damascus to southern Arabia. They all had one point in common marked on their maps, between the Dead Sea and the Gulf of Aqaba, in what is now Jordan. It was an extraordinary crossroads in the kingdom of the Nabataeans: the sculpted city of Petra. With this Semitic town's strategic importance and the taxes the wily herdsmen charged the merchants, the city became a powerful force, to the point that the Nabataean town expanded to become an empire.

At that time Petra had 20,000 inhabitants. A population that lived from the advantages offered by this unique city: security, water and trade. It is surrounded by an impregnable ring of mountains, which became walls for the city itself. Their houses, palaces and tombs were made by boring into the rock, sculpting it to transform it into majestic facades, and emptying out the rock so they could live inside the mountains, or make large cisterns to retain the valuable rainwater.

That splendour lasted for a couple of centuries, but its legend has lasted to this day. Many of those buildings cut into the mountains rouse the admiration of the thousands of people who visit Petra each year, like a pilgrimage to a great wonder. The entrance through the narrow defile of the Siq, the only way in, forms a passageway more than 1.5 km (0.9 mi) long, which at some points is no wider than 2.5 m (8.2 ft) and reaches 100 m (328 ft) in height. It is only accessible by walking or on horseback.

The narrow canyon immediately opens out into a large square that contains one of the most important monuments of the entire complex: El Khazneh Firaum, or the Pharaoh's Treasury. This is an extraordinary building, about 40 m (131 ft) high and 28 m (91 ft) across the front, carved into the mountainside, and still almost intact. Although its origins are lost, legend has it that it was commissioned by a pharaoh who wanted to hide his riches in the urn in the upper part of the building. For centuries, the

↑El Khazneh Firaum Greek in inspiration, Khazneh Firaum is one of the most elaborate and complex structures in Petra.

inhabitants and occupants of Petra in a vain effort fired guns at it, hoping to make jewels and money fall out, until the urn was partly destroyed. The characteristics of the Pharaoh's Treasury are repeated in other monuments in Petra: niches, half-columns standing out from the stone, and crowned by delicate capitals, alcoves and triangular pediments. The interior, on the other hand, is simple: it has just one large hall and one chamber.

More than tombs

Although Petra has many tombs, some clearly for nobles and others for common people, you will also find ordinary houses and other amazing works of architecture, bored out of the rock. All this creativity was feasible thanks to limestone which made it possible to sculpt and drill it, although this required both physical effort and artistic technique.

This system brought about one of the most amazing buildings in Petra: the Monastery. Once you have passed the gorges, the monastery is located on a small and inaccessible plateau. It is an impressive building, 47 m high by 50 m wide (154 by 164 ft), with a grand doorway that is 8 m (26 ft) high. The entire facade and the interior were cut out of the rock in the first century. Inside it has a single hall with a large niche in the back wall and an altar in the middle. The Monastery is originally a Nabataean work, but its name comes from the fact that it was used as a Christian monastery during the Byzantine period.

Nabataean Petra, which initiated the original architecture of the enclave, began to decline from the beginning of Roman domination, felt in the city from the year 106, when it first became part of the Roman

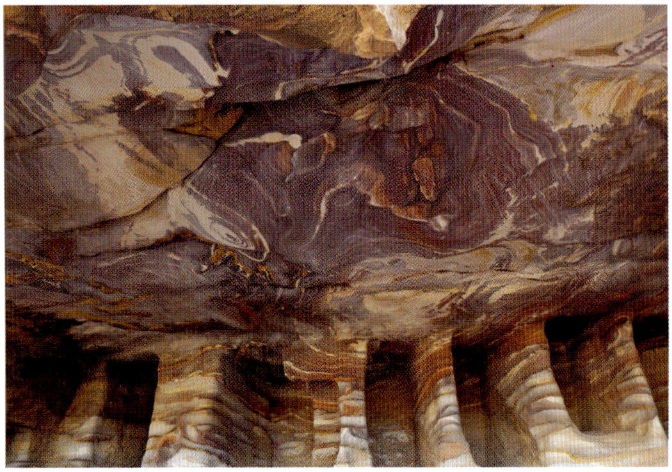

↑The Monastery The size of the seated man in the turret of the Monastery gives a clear idea of the enormous size of the complex.

↑Nabataean Tomb Image of the rock vault inside the halls in the Royal Tombs.

↗The Treasury Through a narrow path, visitors arriving at Petra can just glimpse a few details of El Khazneh Firaum.

→Niches Despite archaeological studies, it has not yet been possible to explain the purpose of the niches cut out of the rock.

province of Arabia. Some later works thus show an Imperial style: the theatre, carved into the rock by the Nabataeans, was rebuilt and enlarged by the Romans to create a space with 33 rows of seats and capacity for 3,000 people. Another Roman feature is the colonnade that crosses the entire central area of Petra, flanked by the markets, and leading to the ruins of the Nabataean temple of Qasr el Blint, in the middle of the sacred area of Temenos.

In 363 an earthquake destroyed half of the city. From then on the population began to fall and its imminent decline ensued. Islamic domination from the 7th century onwards left it a ghost town. For 12 centuries Petra was left lost and lonely in the mountains. It only offered a refuge for Bedouins. In 1812 however, Swiss explorer Johann Ludwig Burckhardt, who had heard rumours of the legendary city, found the hidden site. News of the wonders he saw there began to spread, and made it possible to bring the city back from oblivion.

The Royal Tombs

The Royal Tombs carved into the rocks in Petra stand out thanks to their monumental quality and their colours.

Corinthian Tomb With architecture of Hellenistic influence, it measures 28 m (91 ft) square. It is very damaged due to erosion.

The Palace Tomb This is the largest of them all. Originally it protruded from the rock it was cut from. It stands out because of its columns and its four interior chambers, two of which are connected.

The Silk Tomb So-called for the iridescent tones of its facade, it has the classic Nabataean double cornice, supported by four pillars. It is surrounded by other tombs and funerary chambers.

Apse In the 5th century, the tomb was converted into a church, and two separate niches were connected to make the apse.

Internal courtyard The Urn Tomb was carved into a deep cavity and emptied out to form a patio, 23 m (75 ft) wide with two colonnades on each side.

Urn Tomb The name is taken from a stone urn that crowns the facade. Its three upper windows, at a great height, communicate with independent chambers, presumably to avoid looting.

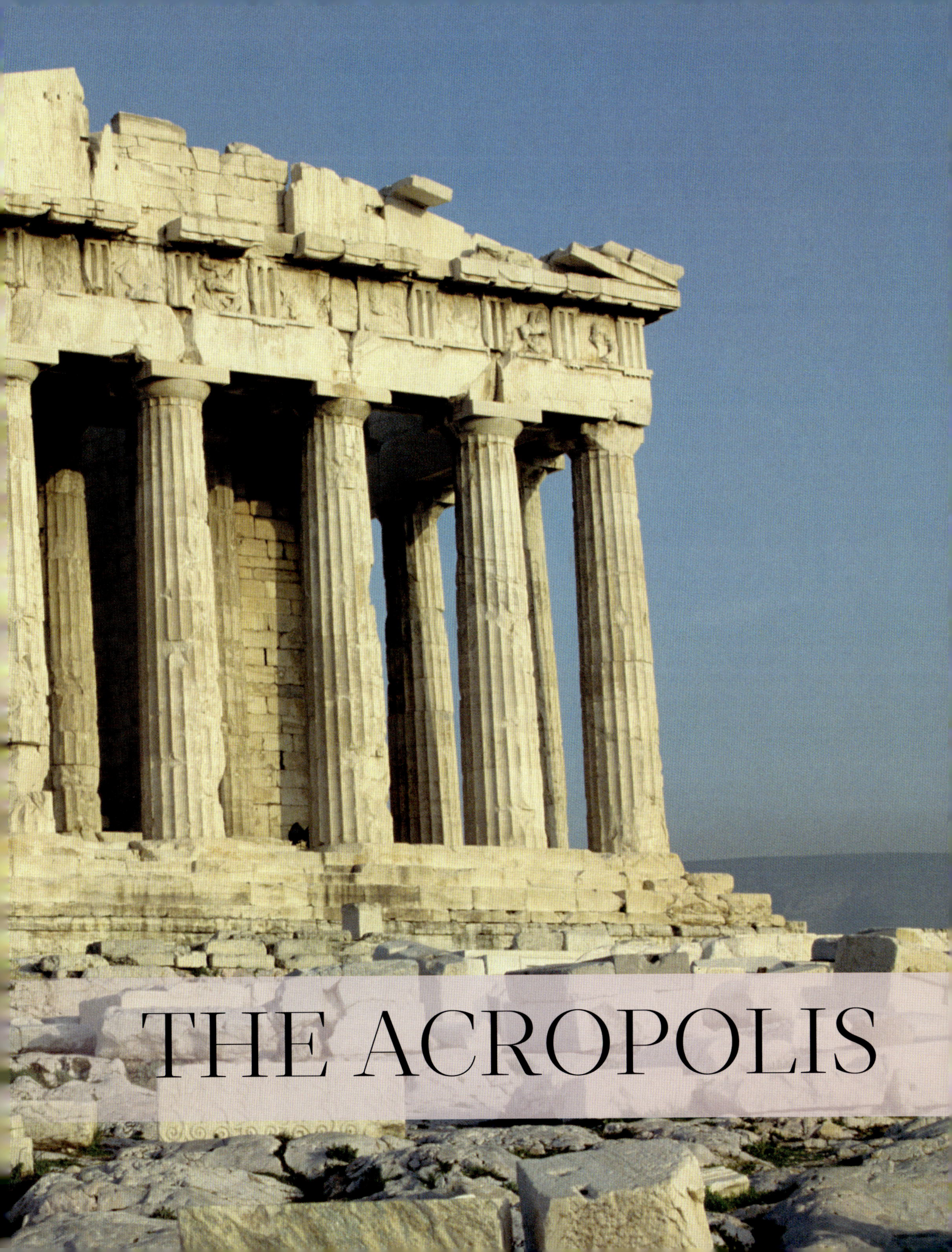

THE ACROPOLIS

Athens It took the architects directed by Phidias nearly half a century to raise the Acropolis on one of the hills of Athens, the capital of Greece.

The jewel of classical Greek art

The temples, statues, gates, friezes and paintings of the Acropolis in Athens are the most perfect testimony to Greek monumental art, conceived during the Golden Age of Pericles.

Situated on a rocky hill, at 156 m (511 ft), the Acropolis in Athens has watched over the city, the port of Piraeus and the horizon of the Aegean for 24 centuries. Its buildings are universal symbols and are the most representative architectural and artistic complex of classical Greece. The Parthenon – the principal temple dedicated to the goddess Athena Parthenos, and a model of the Doric order, the Propylaea – the monumental entrance of the Acropolis, the temple of Athena Nike and the Erechtheion make up the group of four masterpieces united by ornaments and statues inspired by the characters and events of the rich legends of Greek mythology.

Even today, some of the ruins of that ancient splendour survive, and it is worth remembering the words of the historian and essayist Plutarch regarding these monuments: 'Somehow there shines in them a flower of youth that has preserved their appearance over the passage of time. It seems as if these works have a breath that is always alive, and a soul impervious to ageing.'

The Acropolis is a product of its age: the most brilliant and splendid of classical Greece. During the 5th century BC, after the Athenian victory over the Persians, a governor arose that was not only capable in war and politics but had a refined artistic and philosophical profile, Pericles. His rule defined the most brilliant period of Athens. An artistic culture flourished under Pericles' influence, with such members as the philosophers Gorgias and Socrates, the tragedian Aeschylus, the sculptor Polykleitos, the physician Hippocrates, the sculptor Phidias and the architects Mnesicles, Iktinos and Kallikrates, among others. In 447 BC, Phidias turned to these aforementioned architects to realise his dream: to rebuild the ancient Acropolis from the ruins of Mycenaean origin as the culmination of his plan to beautify Athens.

Looking for perfection

Under the direction of Phidias, a very famous sculptor in Athens, the team of architects and artists took 42 years (447–405 BC) to complete the buildings on the

↑Elevation Acropolis means literally 'high city'. The Athens Acropolis stands on a hill that is 156 m (511 ft) high.

Acropolis. The first 15 of those were spent building the Parthenon. Iktinos and Kallikrates took care of the design, a construction model that comes close to architectural perfection: 69 m (226 ft) long, 31 m (101 ft) wide, a little more than 10 m (33 ft) high and with an imposing peristyle made up of eight Doric columns at the front and the back and 15 on each of the sides. The building was complemented by a 12 m (36 ft) statue of Athena, made of marble and some 1,200 kg (2,645 lbs) of gold, which, it is said, served as a guide for mariners approaching Piraeus by sea.

Today it is only the western wing of the building that remains in good condition. The rest has been damaged by earthquakes and wars. The greatest destruction took place during the Turkish occupation, when they used it as a powder magazine. During an attack by the Venetian Fleet in 1687, a bomb exploded inside and left it in ruins. Until then the ornaments and the metopes (the 92 sculptured marble pictures with various mythological episodes) that ran all around the upper frieze of the building had been kept in very good condition. From the surviving sculptures, many (mainly 75 m [246 ft] of frieze and some 15 metopes from the southern side of the temple) were taken to London at the beginning of the 19th century, by order of the British ambassador, Lord Elgin, to be sold to the British Museum, where they are still on display.

At the same time the Propylaea, the gigantic doors of the Acropolis, were removed from the Parthenon. They were also of the Doric order, and were made by the architect Mnesicles between approximately 437 and 431 BC. The other two outstanding temples in the complex are the temple of Athena Nike, designed by Kallikrates, and the Erechtheion, attributed to

↑Temple of Athena Nike Ionic colonnade from this temple dedicated to the winged goddess Athena, a symbol of victory.

↗Caryatids Columns in the shape of women from the portico of the Erechtheion, one of the most iconic images of the Acropolis.

→The complex Aerial view of the complex, where the Parthenon stands out.

↑Theatre of Dionysus Statues sculpted in the proscenium of the Theatre of Dionysus, built in the 4th century BC at the feet of the Acropolis.

Philocles. Both buildings are of the Ionic order and were erected during the Peloponnesian War. However, the Acropolis was finished in time, to endure, up until today, as the most brilliant testimony to the so-called Golden Age of Pericles.

In the 21st century there are two enemies that menace the Acropolis. One is environmental pollution, especially from cars which corrodes marble. Greek technicians are using laser techniques to clean marble statues, friezes and reliefs, and, in some cases, so recover their original polychrome colours. The second enemy is the restoration carried out a century ago by the architect Balanos, who decided to fix the large blocks of marble that were in danger of falling by drilling through them and inserting braces and brackets made of iron. In time the marble has cracked and become stained by rust. For some years now you will have seen a large crane on the Parthenon. It is specially designed to lift out these blocks, so the iron brackets can be changed for others made of non-degradable titanium.

The splendour of Athens

In addition to the main temples, the Acropolis also contained other buildings and statues dedicated to Greek deities.

Erechtheion This Ionic order temple has the portico of the Caryatids on its facade.

Athena Promachos This lost statue of the goddess in combat was made of bronze and measured between 6 and 15 m in height (between 20 and 50 ft).

The Propylaea This was the entrance to the complex. Made in marble, it was composed of various spaces, supported by Doric columns.

Temple of Athena Nike Dedicated to Athena the Victorious, it has an almost square plan with Ionic order columns and a frieze with episodes from the Median Wars.

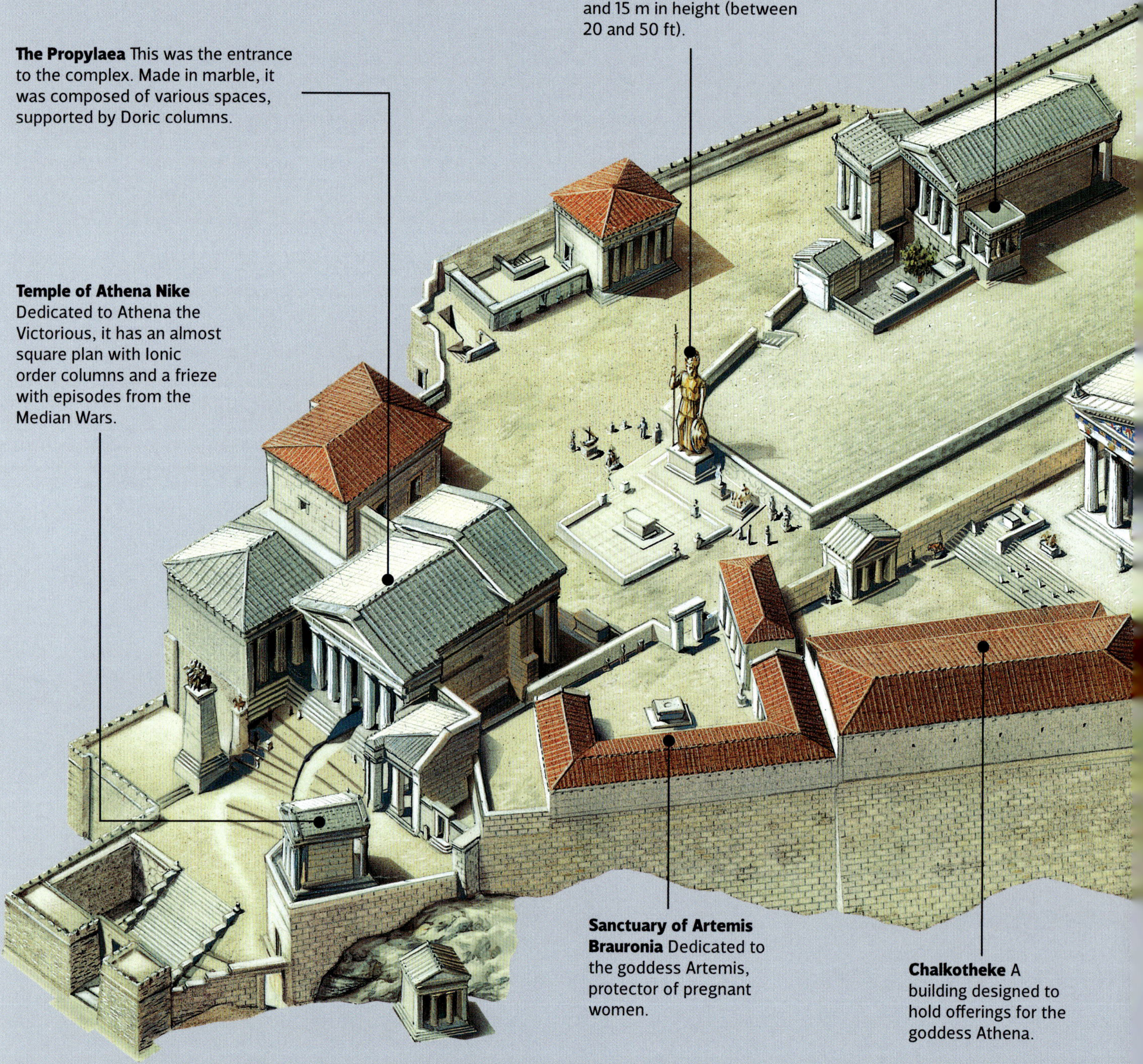

Sanctuary of Artemis Brauronia Dedicated to the goddess Artemis, protector of pregnant women.

Chalkotheke A building designed to hold offerings for the goddess Athena.

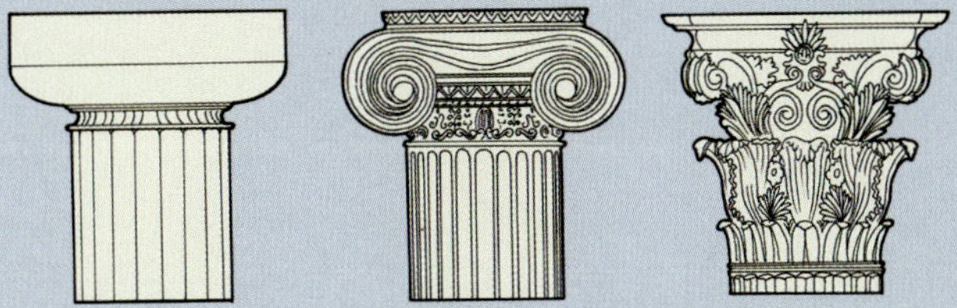

The classical orders Classical architecture was governed by three orders with different principles, the objective being to obtain harmonious proportions. They can be identified by their columns. From left to right, capitals for the Doric, Ionian and Corinthian orders.

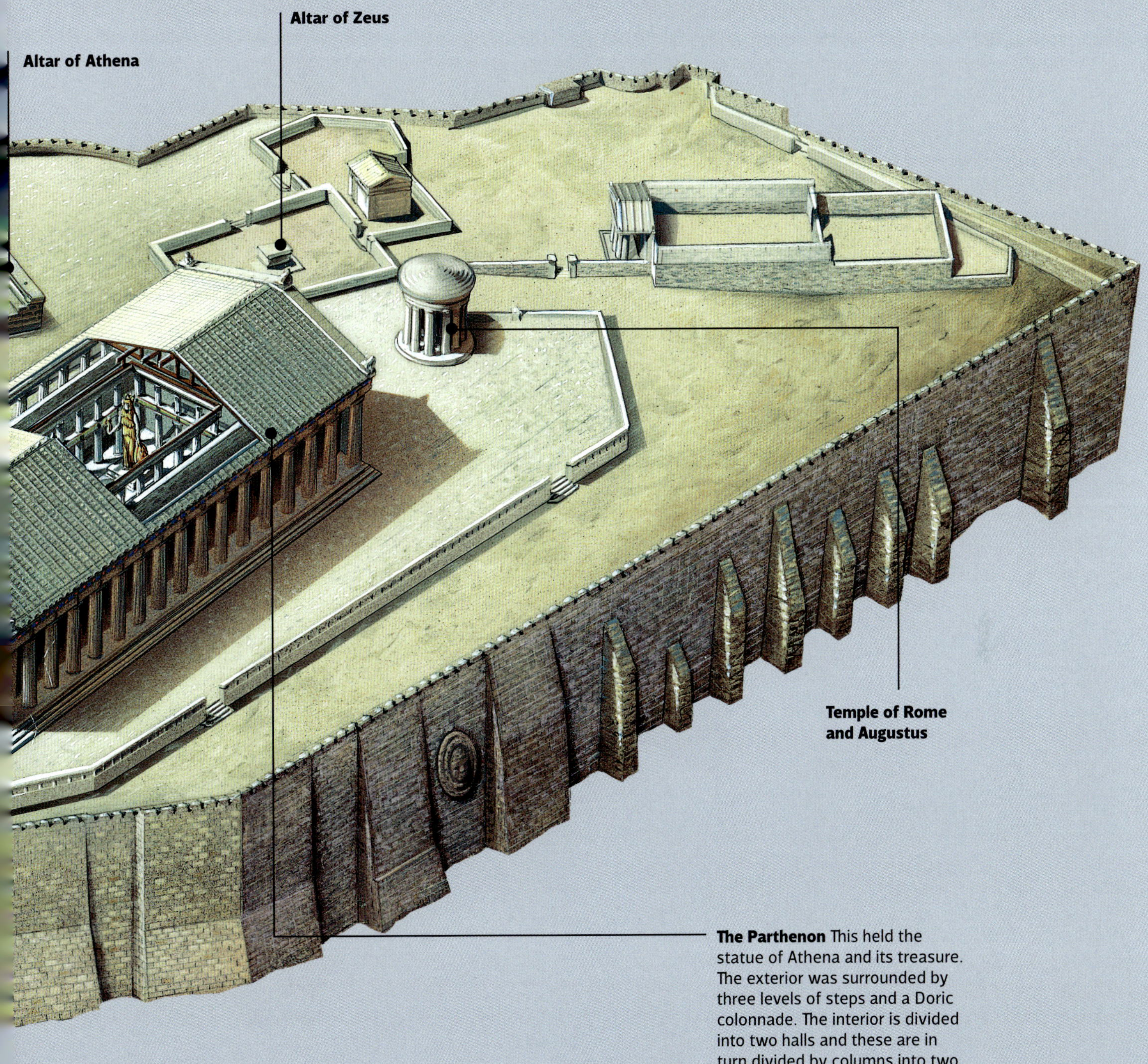

The Parthenon This held the statue of Athena and its treasure. The exterior was surrounded by three levels of steps and a Doric colonnade. The interior is divided into two halls and these are in turn divided by columns into two separate naves.

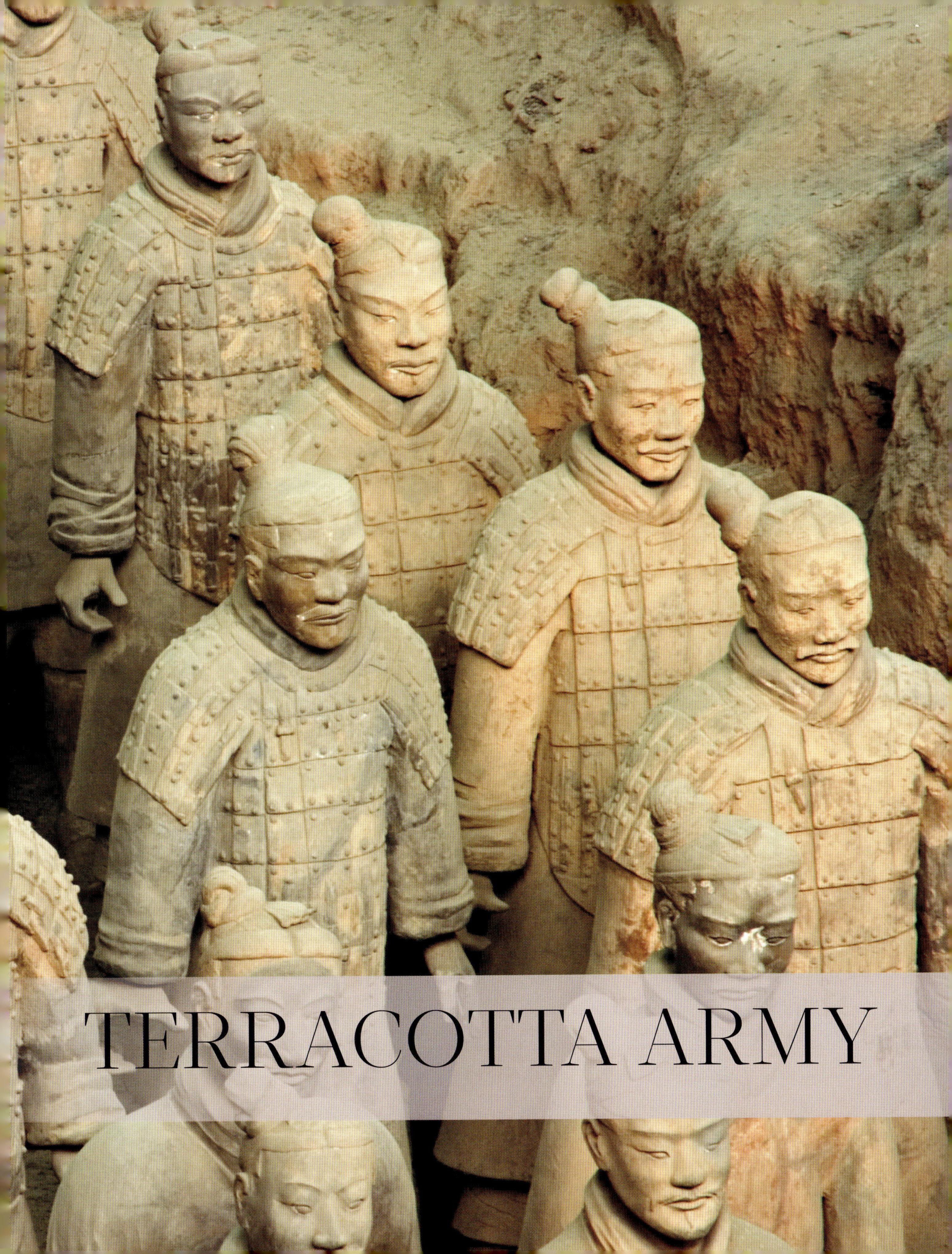

TERRACOTTA ARMY

Xian This impressive army stands inside the Mausoleum of Qin Shi Huang, near the city of Xian in Shaanxi province.

A clay army

Thousands of life-size figures made from clay with exquisite detail more than 2,200 years ago have put the Chinese city of Xian on the artistic map of the world.

A marvel that remained hidden for 22 centuries. Perhaps that is why in 1974 people were so amazed when this army of thousands of clay warriors was discovered: an army buried on its feet and in battle order, close to the tomb of the first emperor of China, Qin Shi Huang (260–210 BC). Together with the tomb of Tutankhamen, experts consider it the most important archaeological find of the 20th century.

The soldiers are ranged in formation, in corridors that are separated from each other by earth walls. The formations, rectangular, faithfully reproduce their battle formation: at the front there are three rows of archers, then the light infantry and finally the heavy infantry, with soldiers in plate armour, and then the cavalry. Near these first three trenches, another smaller one was found later containing some 90 suits of scale armour for men and horses, and 40 helmets. Some of these were made with sheets of limestone, wired together with copper. Even though they have often lost their colour, scientists say that they were originally painted to imitate the leather armour that soldiers of the time really wore. Looking at these facts and at the number of warriors, historians speculate that the terracotta army may be nothing less than an exact reproduction of the imperial guard of Qin Shi Huang.

Imperial China

The first emperor of China held a war of unification against various feudal kingdoms which shared power and territory in the China of the 3rd century BC. His victory and conquest over the other feudal lords in 221 BC meant the creation of the first dynasty with absolute power of the entire country: the Qin dynasty.

Qin Shi Huang died in 210 BC. However, obsessed by power and immortality, from the first day of his mandate he began to prepare, in secret, this underground world which would surround his tomb and protect it symbolically after his death. More than 38 years and 700,000 workers were necessary for the

↑Reconstruction All the figures are subjected to a careful restoration process.

↗Orientation The army is oriented towards the east, from where it was supposed that the spirits of the conquered kingdoms would come to seek their revenge.

construction of this terracotta city, located 30 km (18.6 mi) to the east of the city of Xian, the capital of his empire.

A complex process of modelling

The figures were made in series, with moulds for the heads, torsos and limbs, which were assembled to make the figures after the clay was baked. The noses, ears and hair were modelled on individual sheets of clay to give individual and personalised features to each figure. In the same way, a terracotta covering was made to form the details of the uniforms and the armour, which were painted with lacquer-based paint after baking to look realistic.

During the years after the amazing discovery of the soldiers, the excavations continued, and other trenches were found with different figures and objects, which gave rise to the theory that the emperor had recreated his entire cultural universe in these galleries. In the so-called bronze chariot trench, two complete and perfectly made examples were found to support this theory. In recent years other discoveries have been: the trench of the officials, the trench of the cavalry and the western stables, and the trench of bronze birds, with figures of water birds, such as a crane with a worm in its beak, all with astonishing realism and beauty.

The teams of archaeologists who participate in the excavation have estimated that it will need about one hundred years of work to dig through the entire site.

↑Battle The terracotta army was buried according to a scheme of battle order.

→Stature The average height of the soldiers is 1.80 m (6 ft), although the statues of high military rank are rather taller.

↑Colours The last warriors to be discovered confirm that they were painted in bright colours.

↗Details Each figure was made to be unique, with amazing detail and realism.

They also think that it will certainly become one of the most important archaeological sites in the world during the 21st century.

The unexplored tomb

The only place that has been identified but not yet investigated is the Emperor's tomb itself. According to the *Memoirs* of the Chinese historian Sima Qian, the tomb of Qin Shi Huang was filled with objects that were both materially and symbolically valuable. The roof was painted with a representation of the heavenly constellations and the floor reproduced the Earth, with the principal Chinese rivers simulated by streams of flowing mercury thanks to mechanical devices that took them towards a miniature ocean. However, all this is only literary conjecture, with as yet no scientific foundation. So far the Chinese authorities have specifically refused to begin the process that would lead to the opening of the tomb until there are scientific guarantees that ensure the process will avoid the deterioration or destruction of the treasures that lie within.

The Emperor's Mausoleum

The terracotta army forms part of the funerary compound of Qin Shi Huang, which includes a grandiose mausoleum, much of which remains to be discovered.

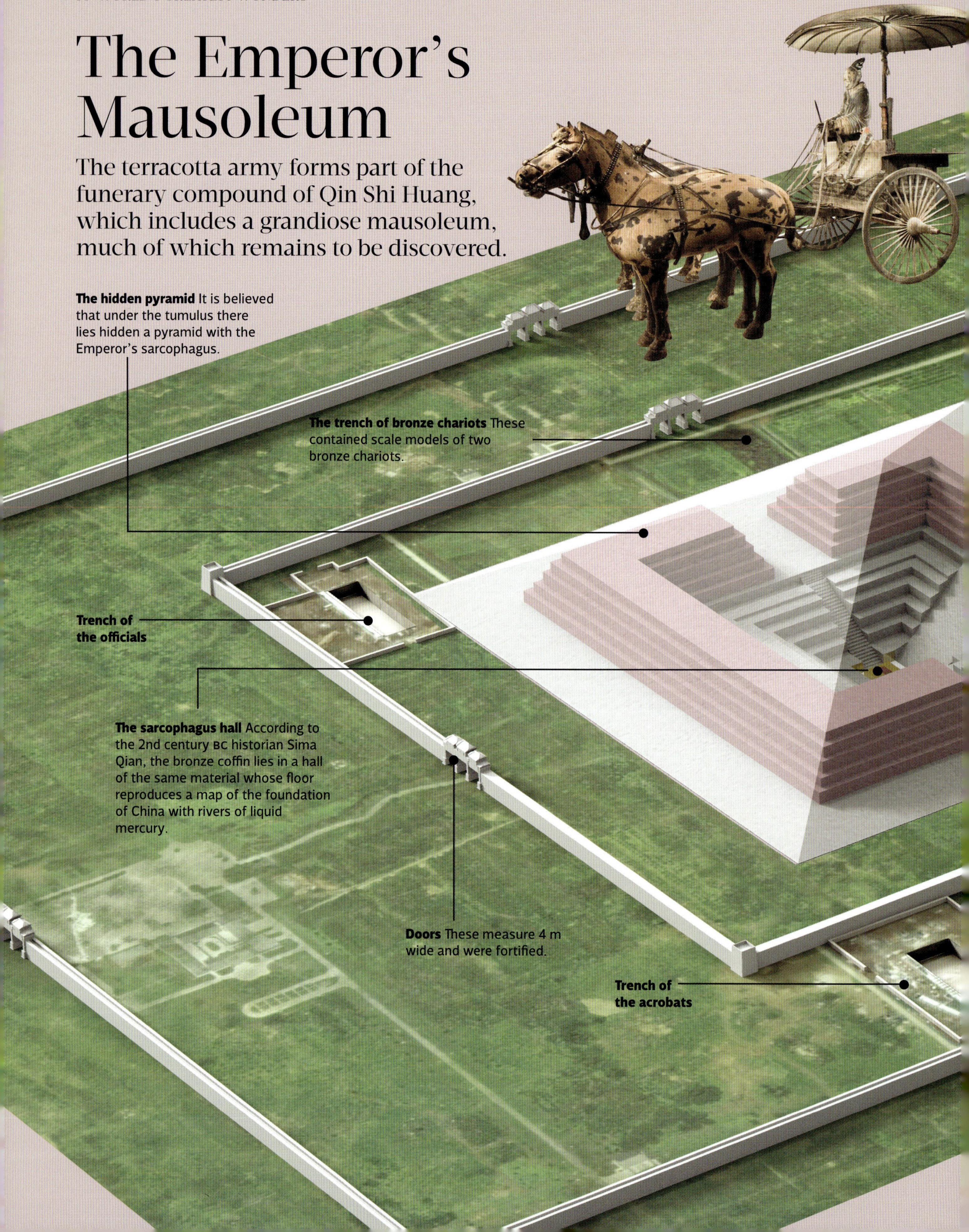

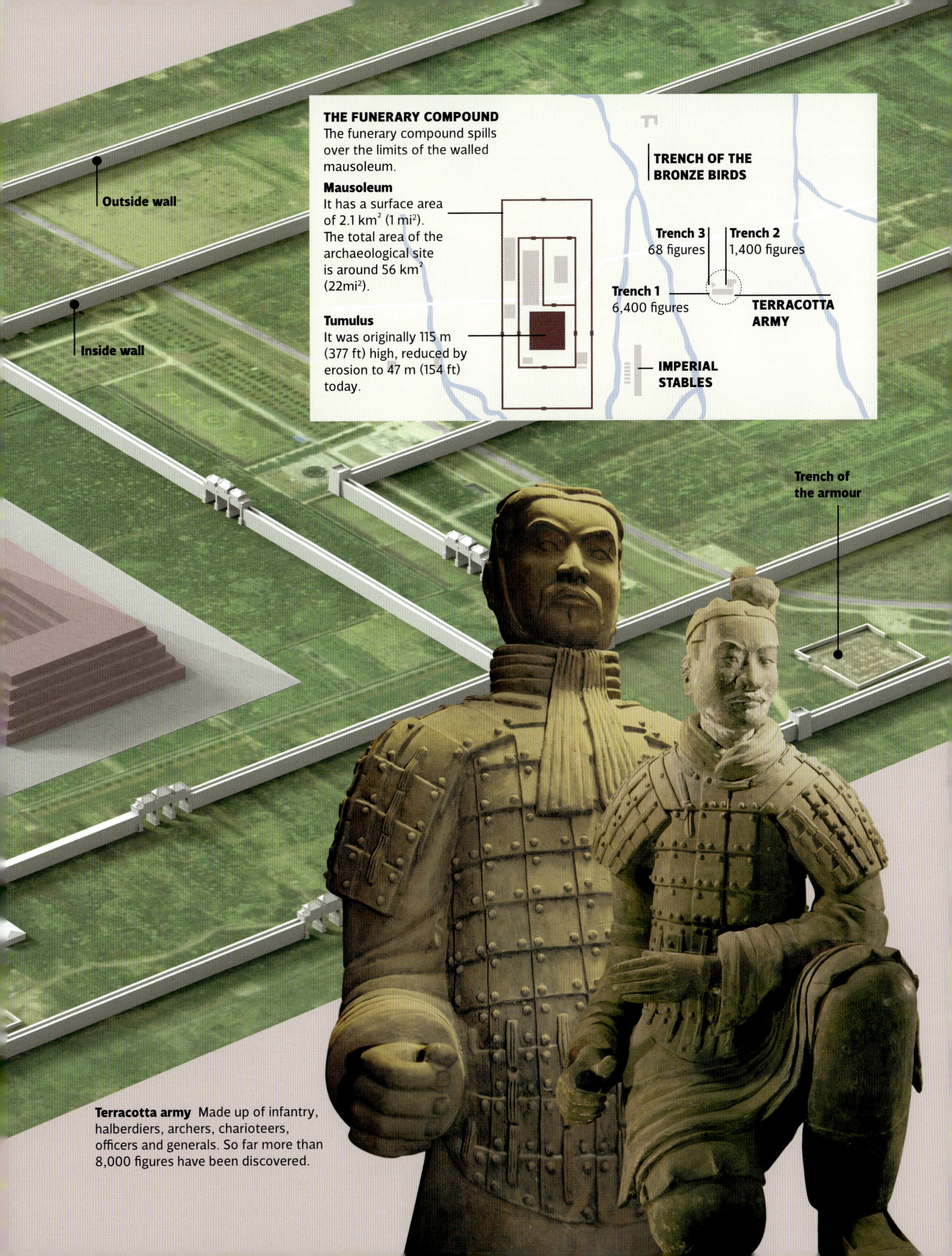

Terracotta army Made up of infantry, halberdiers, archers, charioteers, officers and generals. So far more than 8,000 figures have been discovered.

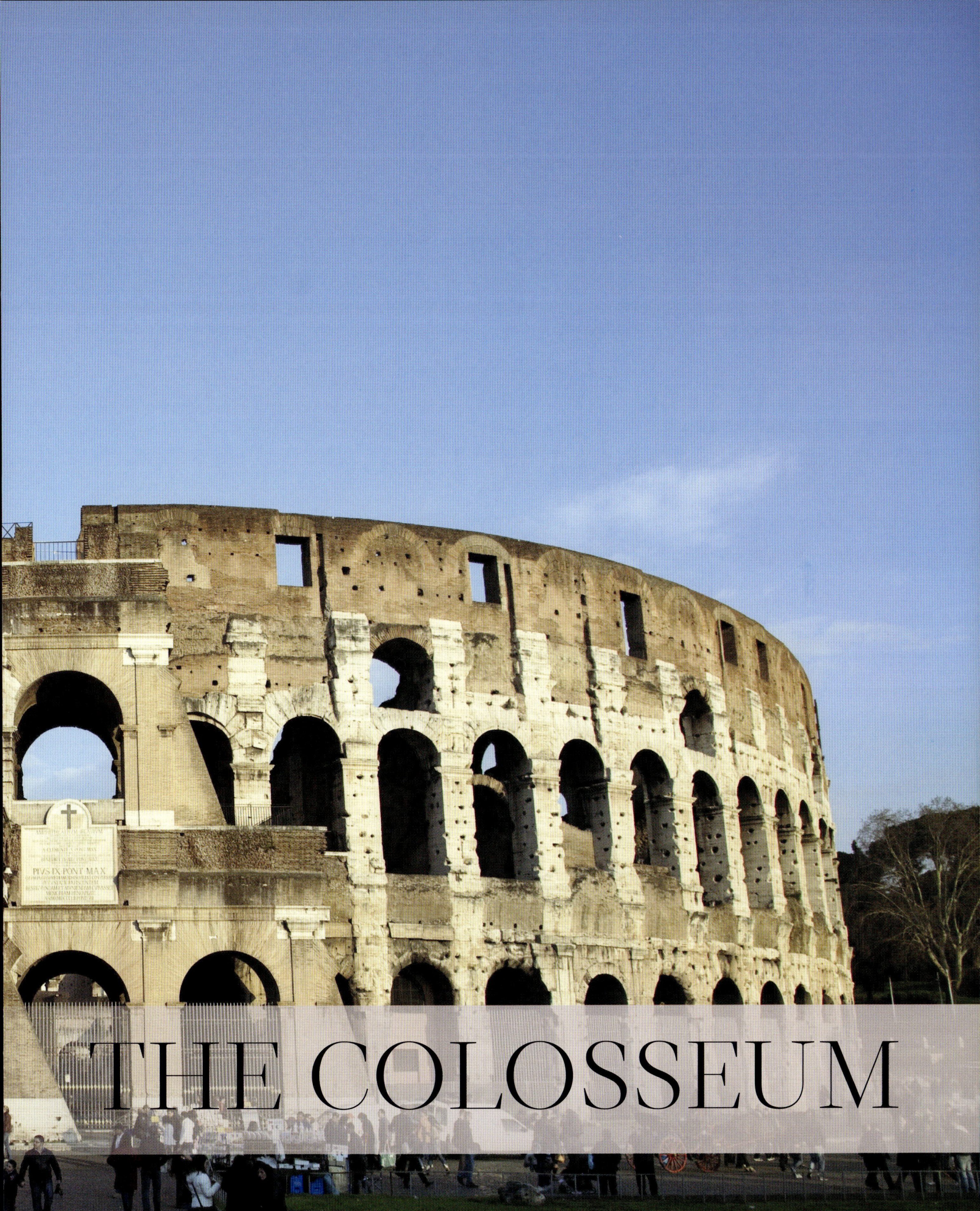

THE COLOSSEUM

Rome The capital of Italy is a city full of monuments, but few attract as many visitors as the ruins of the ancient Colosseum, built nearly two thousand years ago.

A monument to engineering

The Flavian Amphitheatre is Rome's most emblematic building, and is one of the living testimonies to the Roman Empire, to the values of its architecture and engineering, and a reminder of its customs.

In almost 20 centuries of existence it has been an amphitheatre, execution ground, artificial lake, scene of fights to the death, sacred site, fortress, quarry and example of Roman architecture, until finding its current role as a worldwide icon and emblem of the city of Rome, and one of its most visited tourist attractions. The unmistakable outline of the semi-ruined stadium is an image that is recognised the world over. The Flavian amphitheatre, better known as the Colosseum, sitting in the heart of modern Rome, has other similar monuments as neighbours, such as the Imperial Fora, The Arch of Constantine, the buildings on the nearby Palatine Hill and, a few blocks further to the south, the Circus Maximus. But it has always exerted a stronger fascination than the other monuments. The stories told about its history are sometimes mixed with legend. During its heyday bloody Roman spectacles were held in its arena: from animal fights (venationes) to gladiator fights (munera); from reconstructions of naval battles (naumachiae) to executions of prisoners using wild animals (noxii).

Despite its considerable capacity – 45,000 people, in 80 rows of steps – it wasn't called the Colosseum for its size, but for a huge statue of Nero that stood close by. During his reign, the area surrounding the Colosseum caught fire and burned down in the year 64. Nero then confiscated it for his personal use. He built his magnificent residence, the Domus Aurea, there, with an artificial lake, plus gardens and porticos. The main gate of the residence was guarded by the giant bronze statue, the Colossus of Nero. After his death, the Empire found stability under the reign of Vespasian, who recovered these lands and built an enormous amphitheatre, probably with the proceeds from the booty of his victorious military campaign in Judea in the year 70. Building the circus took more than eight years; it was inaugurated by Titus, the son and successor of Vespasian, in the year 80, one year after his father's death.

An enormous building

Years later, when the fourth upper gallery was completed, the amphitheatre was converted into an

↑Combined styles The outside combines the Doric order on the first level, Ionic on the second and Corinthian on the third, giving great overall beauty to the complex.

↗From the air Aerial view of a detail of the great Roman amphitheatre.

enormous oval building 189 m long, 156 m wide and 57 m high (620 by 511 by 187 ft). The evident similarities show that the Colosseum inspired the design of many sports stadiums in the 20th century, among other reasons because the distribution of its internal galleries, with a great number of concentric steps connected together, allowed rapid entry and exit by the public. The wooden floor that covered the arena for fights has not survived, so you can see the labyrinth of underground dungeons used to hold prisoners, gladiators and wild animals. In a bravura display of engineering, there was even a thin cloth cover that was moved by a network of ropes worked by long poles. Even though it has been taken to be a model of the Roman architectural genius, its style, which mixes orders (Doric, Tuscan, Ionic and Corinthian) superimposed in its galleries, was not usual.

Earthquakes and lightning strikes have made cracks in its structure, although it continued functioning until the 6th century. The last gladiator fight took place in about 435, while the wild animal hunt shows carried on until the year 523. A little later its splendour failed, and it was lost in the darkness of the middle ages. Like many other public buildings, it fell into the hands of the Church, which lacked the funds to maintain it. This meant that whenever natural catastrophes struck the city, the Colosseum suffered irreparable damage. The greatest destruction came with the earthquake of 1349, which damaged its structure and damaged the upper galleries of the southern side, leaving them with their current appearance.

↑Arena The central area was an oval surface of 187 x 55 m (613 x 176 ft), protected by walls 5 m (16 ft) high.

←Imperial Rome View of the Colosseum sitting in the urban surrounding of the city.

↗The structure The arches of the edifice are made of travertine rock and no mortar was used to build them.

↑Underground For a few years now it has been possible to visit the wild animal cages and the cells for the prisoners in the cellars.

In the middle of this stage of obscurity, the Colosseum was a ruin, dismissed and plundered by the Romans themselves. A popular saying in Rome says 'What the Barbarians couldn't do, the Barberini did instead.' This means that the Barbarian invasions of Rome in the 5th century were less destructive than the plundering of stone and marble by the Barberini, among other noble families, to build their palaces and other private buildings.

It was Pope Benedict IV who put a stop to this free use of the stones of the Colosseum in 1749, when he declared that the building was a sacred site, in homage to the Christian martyrs who had been executed there. However, this version was later seen as a legend and began to lose strength, seeing as the majority of the Christians massacred during the official persecution of the Empire fell in the Circus Maximus. Thus the Colosseum was retained as a pagan symbol, although that Christian past is remembered in the tradition maintained by all the Popes of celebrating the Stations of the Cross inside the Colosseum each year during Holy Week.

The great Roman amphitheatre

The Colosseum is amazing above all for its perfect structure and the technical innovations it incorporated.

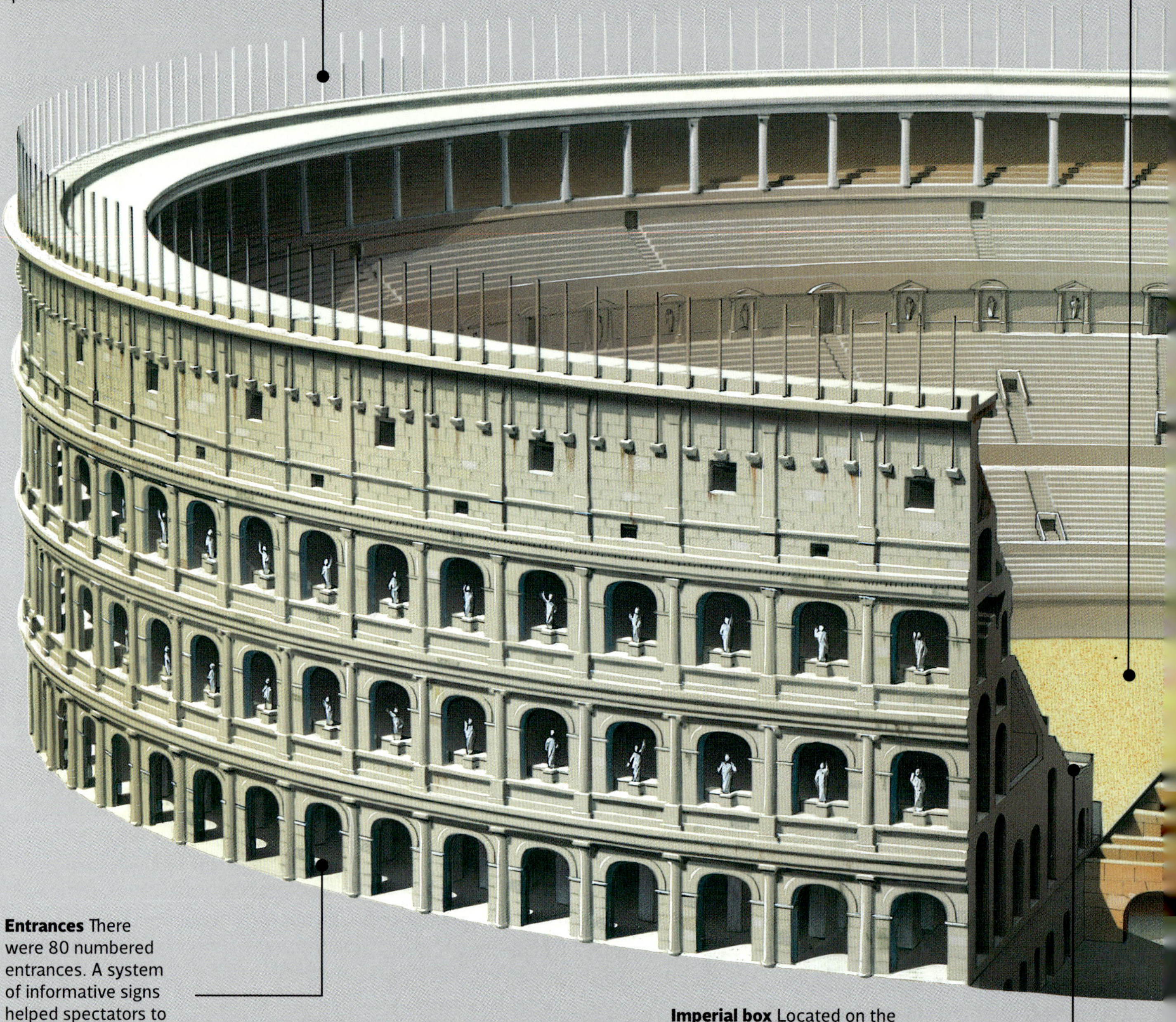

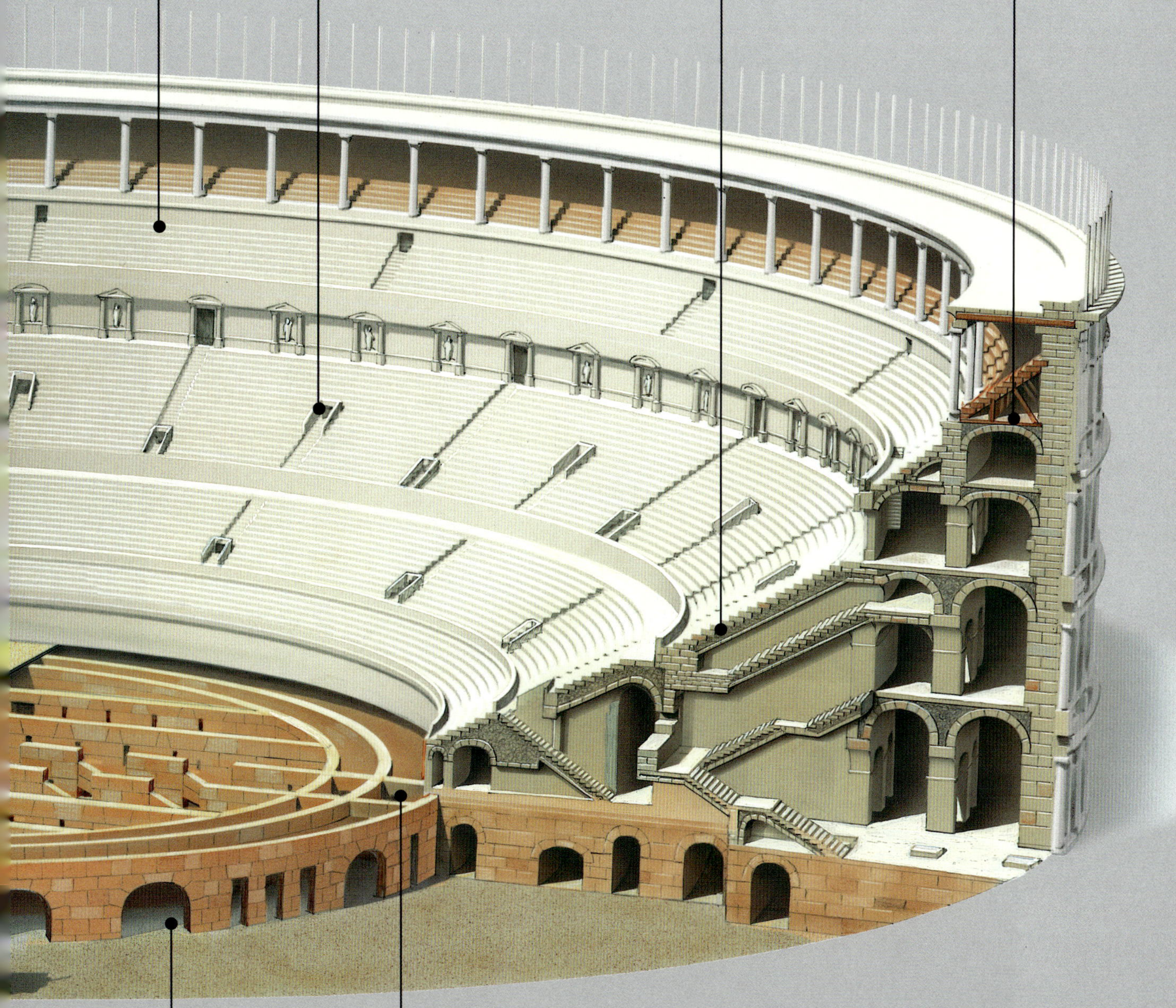
Terraces On the highest part the seats were made of wood, and seated women, slaves, and foreigners. The first three terraces were reserved for Roman nobles and wealthy citizens, and their seats were made of marble.
Stairs The stairs lead from the concentric galleries on the ground floor to the upper levels.
Vomitoria These exits made it possible to empty the amphitheatre in only three minutes.
Internal configuration It was built on the basis of several arcades vaulted in Roman concrete, brick and stone.
Wild animal cellars
Gladiators' passageway

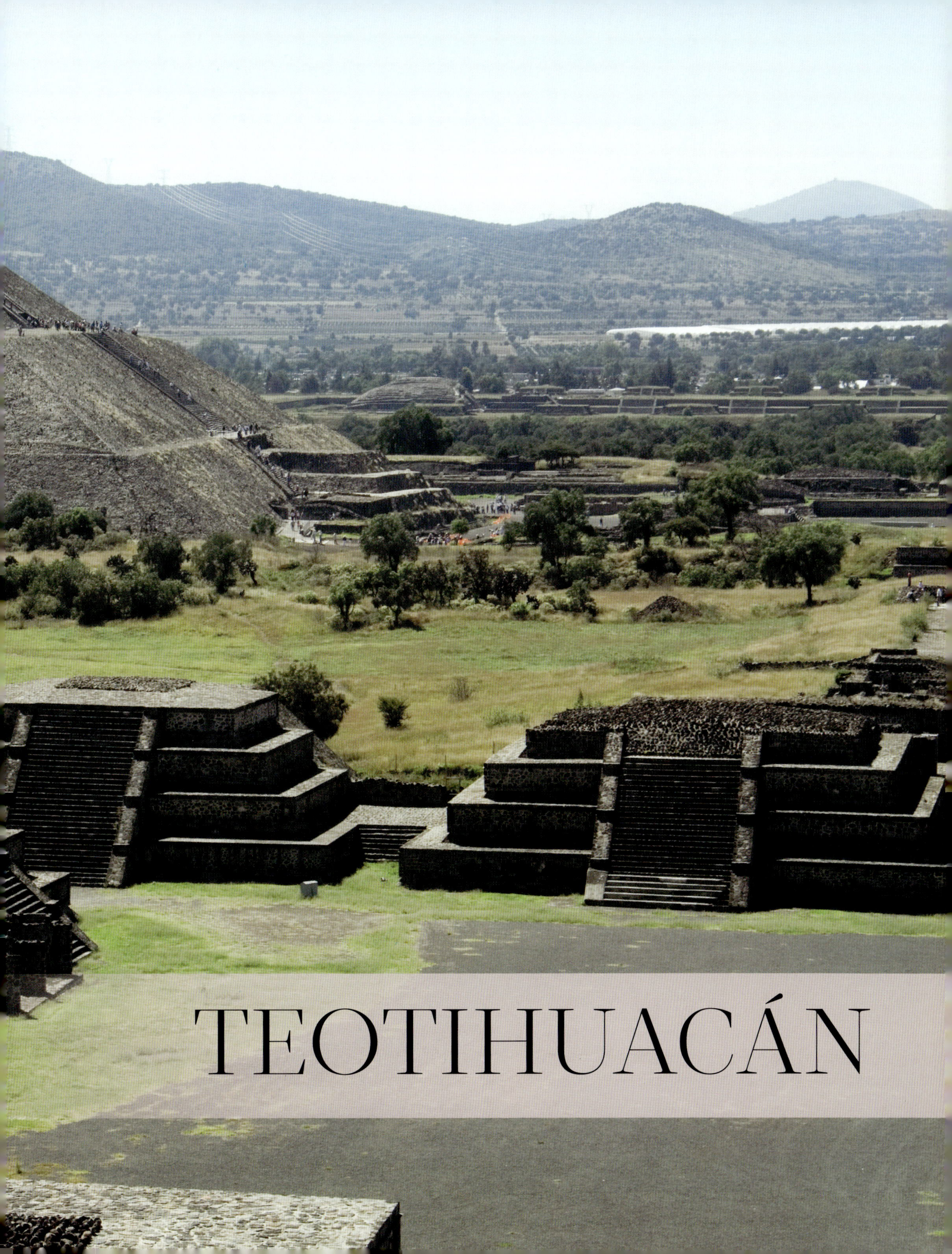

TEOTIHUACÁN

Teotihuacán The most influential city of Pre-Hispanic America is located in the modern city of the same name, 45 km (28 mi) from Mexico City.

The largest pre-Hispanic city

The great Mesoamerican city of antiquity guards the mystery of its origin and its purpose, but its ruins are proof of the splendour that for 500 years elevated it to the status of house of the gods.

Enclosed in the north-eastern corner of the valley of Mexico, some 45 km (28 mi) from Mexico City's Federal District, the 'City where the gods were born', its name in the náhuatl language, was a neolithic conglomerate of isolated houses dating from the 3rd century BC. It was not a particularly important site in the life of the area, however, for unknown reasons, four centuries later a splendid period began which would last half a millennium.

Some archaeologists speculate that Teotihuacán had been converted into a religious centre of high cultural level, which influenced neighbouring cities. This is supposed to have attracted thousands of people from other regions to move in and participate in its religious ceremonies. And it was mainly the buildings dedicated to religion that helped convert the city into a marvel of monuments. A living testimony is the wide Avenue of the Dead, which forms the city's central axis, 4 km long and 40 m wide (2 mi by 131 ft), dominating the current archaeological site and flanked by several hundred temples and tombs.

The Avenue of the Dead surprises visitors today mainly thanks to its four most outstanding monuments: the Pyramid of the Moon, the Pyramid of the Sun, the Palace of Quetzalpapálotl and the Temple of Quetzalcóatl. The Pyramid of the Moon, located at the northern end of the avenue, is made up of four superimposed bodies and under its base is a series of galleries and rooms which are ancient cult sites. Its location is far from random: underground water runs under the pyramid, which in ancient times was related to fertility rituals. These were associated with another divinity that is seen many times around the city, the god Tláloc, lord of rain and fertility. The Plaza of the Moon opens in front of the pyramid and around it, over time, large palaces and temples were built which were occupied by the priests.

One building that has endured is the palace of Quetzalpapálotl (a mythological being, half parrot and half butterfly), whose rooms are supported by pillars decorated with bas-reliefs and its walls painted with symbolic religious subjects.

↑Pyramid of the Sun The tallest building of the sacred city of Teotihuacán. It is illuminated by the sun during the equinox.

But the grandest monument that can be seen on the present-day archaeological site is the Pyramid of the Sun, on the eastern edge of the Avenue of the Dead. It is the highest pyramid in the city and the second highest in Mesoamerica, after the one at Cholula. It is orientated to indicate the rising and setting of the sun and also shows the equinoxes. In its highest part, 64 m (210 ft) up, there is a sanctuary, while under its base there is a gallery of underground tunnels where there are rooms used for ritual purposes.

Heyday and splendour from the 2nd century

These buildings and the rest of the city began their heyday in the 2nd century. Since then, perhaps favoured by the migration of the inhabitants of Cuicuilco, after a volcanic eruption destroyed their city, the development of Teotihuacán was spectacular. It held around 170,000 inhabitants and covered a developed area of 24 km^2 (9.3 mi^2). According to some studies, it would have been the sixth largest city in the world at that time.

Between 300 and 500 AD thousands of houses were built. There were compounds to house family groups of between 60 and 100 people. These large houses were organised in a city plan that was very similar to those of today; a grid organised around two main axes: the Avenue of the Dead, running north–south, and another wide avenue, of similar size, running east–west. The four quadrants that were created were dominated by the residences of the priests and the governors in the central part and by numerous residential quarters towards the edges of the grid. Around the city, more than 9,500 hectares (23,700 acres) were under cultivation. Thousands of craftsmen, artists and tradesmen occupied special areas, creating districts. In these districts they created their refined crafts: making vases, masks in

↑Warrior One of the wall paintings of the palace of Atetelco, one of the residential quarters that surround the sacred complex.

↗Reliefs Representations of gods and sacred animals like serpents and jaguars and the quetzal itself are repeated on the walls of the complex.

↑Avenue of the Dead View from the Pyramid of the Moon of the great avenue that crosses the ceremonial centre.

↗Quetzalpapálotl The columns of the Palace of Butterflies are decorated with rich bas-reliefs.

→Temple of Quetzalcóatl Associated with the God of the Feathered Serpent, his figure appears on various walls of the building, together with others of the god Tlaloc.

stone and ceramics, jewellery made of hard stones, and textiles that were exported to other Mesoamerican towns through abundant commercial trade.

Remains that still surprise today

Part of this art can still be seen in the Palace of Quetzalcóatl, the God of the Feathered Serpent, located in the terrain of the old city. This is a plot of 400 m (1,312 ft) on each side, where the governing caste was concentrated. The Palace of the Feathered Serpent, whose cult was later adopted by the Toltecs and the Aztecs, has sculptures, bas-reliefs and paintings of great beauty and delicacy, still with a few traces of the original polychrome finish. With the same mystery with which it arose and grew, Teotihuacán finished up declining in the 8th and 9th centuries. It may have been due to a Toltec invasion from northern Mexico, but that is far from certain. Not even the Aztecs could resolve the dilemma as they stood in amazement before its magnificent and recent ruins one century before the Spanish reached Mexico.

The city of the gods

The remains of the ceremonial centre of Teotihuacán give an approximate idea of the grandeur once enjoyed by this Mesoamerican city.

Atetelco This walled district is distinguished by murals with military themes.

Temple of the Feathered Serpent Associated with the god Quetzalcóatl, it was built between 100 and 350 AD.

The citadel Its 160,000 m² (1,722,000 ft²) make us think that it must have been the residence of the city's high leaders. It was built around 200 BC, and held important religious buildings and a central shrine.

THE EVOLUTION OF THE BIG CITY	
Origin	200 BC
Period of greatest splendour	3rd and 4th centuries
Extension	24 km (15 mi)
Inhabitants	170,000
Fall	700–800 AD

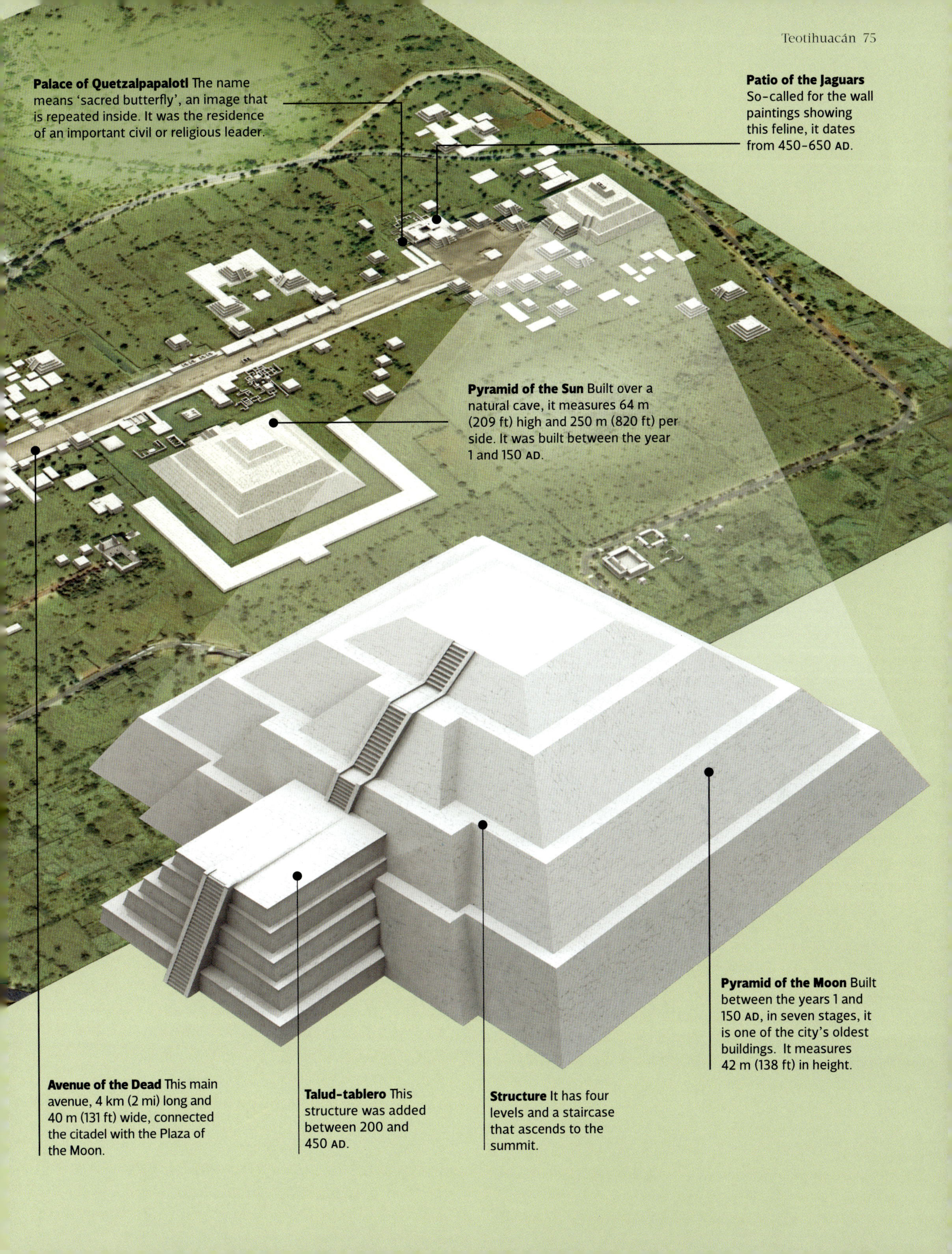
Palace of Quetzalpapalotl The name means 'sacred butterfly', an image that is repeated inside. It was the residence of an important civil or religious leader.
Patio of the Jaguars So-called for the wall paintings showing this feline, it dates from 450–650 AD.
Pyramid of the Sun Built over a natural cave, it measures 64 m (209 ft) high and 250 m (820 ft) per side. It was built between the year 1 and 150 AD.
Pyramid of the Moon Built between the years 1 and 150 AD, in seven stages, it is one of the city's oldest buildings. It measures 42 m (138 ft) in height.
Avenue of the Dead This main avenue, 4 km (2 mi) long and 40 m (131 ft) wide, connected the citadel with the Plaza of the Moon.
Talud-tablero This structure was added between 200 and 450 AD.
Structure It has four levels and a staircase that ascends to the summit.

NAZCA LINES

Nazca These huge outlines can be seen on the arid Nazca plains of south-east Peru.

Mysterious figures

The huge drawings, geometric figures and long lines that are still visible on the desert floor of the Nazca pampas are the wonderful and mysterious legacy of a great civilisation.

For more than five centuries the Nazca Lines have defied human imagination. Drawings of giants, mysterious signs, emblems of superior minds, astral calendar markings, religious liturgy... The almost 2,000 lines and 800 geoglyphs, many of which are still visible on the floor of this arid region, have given birth to various scientific theories and misconceived explanations.

The Nazca culture disappeared from the face of the earth 1,400 years ago. These indigenous people inhabited a region in Peru, around 450 km (280 mi) south of modern-day Lima, between the Pacific coast and the Andean highlands. There, in a region of desert plains, the Nazca created thousands of figures on the floor, seemingly designed to be seen from the sky, as if they were ritual messages to the culture's gods asking for water; or perhaps as if they were large astral markings to mark seasons and planting and harvesting periods... In reality, the purpose of these lines and drawings remains a mystery to this day.

The long straights that were traced almost perfectly, often measuring a number of miles, are almost blemish free. And no less astounding are the geoglyphs of animals, which are more or less proportionate, given their huge size. The Nazca people demonstrated a significant understanding of geometry that allowed them to transfer small-scale figures to large-scale grids that they reproduced on the earth, traced with stakes and cords, depending on the area on which the geoglyph was to be inscribed.

The first discoveries

The lines were first studied at the beginning of the 20th century, when archaeologist Julio Tello carried out scientific research. However, Spanish conquistador Pedro Cieza de León had already mentioned their presence in 1547; he was the first to document 'markings in certain parts of the desert that surrounds Nazca'. However, the references made by Spanish explorers in the 16th and 17th centuries had to wait for a further three centuries before they were 'rediscovered'. The research completed by Tello, and those that followed, confirmed that the Nazca

↑The monkey This is one of the most famous figures, measuring over 100 m (328 ft).

made use of the different and contrasting colour tones of the surface stones and the underlying soil on the desert floor. They removed the surface stones, leaving grooves of exposed yellow-coloured soil. Apparently, this task was performed by hand, as no evidence of animal use has ever been found.

Seen from a great height, the lines of differing lengths overlap and form different geometric shapes: triangles, trapezoids, zigzags and even spirals. Some look like long airport runways, which from a height of 200 m (656 ft) can be appreciated in their full glory. The geoglyphs comprise a veritable collection of different animal shapes: spider, monkey, whale, llama, snake, lizard, dog and several birds. The shapes differ in size, thus it is possible to discern a 180-m (591 ft) long lizard, whilst, amongst the 18 bird figures that can be seen from the air, the hummingbird measures 97 m (318 ft) in length whereas the flamingo measures 275 m (935 ft). Interestingly, several of the anthropomorphic figures, such as the man with a halo, are located on mountainsides; it is therefore easier to see them, especially from a high viewpoint. Many of the figures and lines represented in the geoglyphs are similar in design to decorative motifs found on pottery remains and on traditional embroidery found in the area, as though they were converted into a giant open-air inscription.

The puzzle of interpreting the lines traced on the desert is compounded by another mystery: how have the majority remained visible, considering they were completed between approximately the 2nd and 5th century BC? The response accepted by most scientists has been the region's climate. The plains on which the geoglyphs and lines are found enjoy an average temperature of 25 degrees and very little humidity, a location that is actually

↑Lines The purpose and meaning of these large avenues, similar to aircraft runways, are unknown.

↗Depth The lines are less than 30 cm (12 in) deep, but remain visible thanks to the region's climate.

→Anthropomorphic figures As they are located on mountainsides, they are visible from ground level.

↑Pottery The patterns on Nazca pottery are similar to those of the Nazca lines.

one of the driest on the planet. Furthermore, a unique phenomenon has contributed to their conservation: wind erosion of the surface is limited by the hot air that rises from the earth, which redirects the wind. Under these climatic conditions, the plains' soil is converted into a kind of permanent blackboard: whatever is written on its face can last for centuries. As a result of this arid climate, some archaeologists have maintained the belief that the geoglyphs were a type of offering or the result of a ritual to call for water, most probably in the form of rain. This assumption is supported by the interpretation of a number of findings: in the area surrounding many of the giant drawings, buried offerings have been found, such as marine animals and agricultural produce.

Although the Nazca left no written testimony, their civilisation achieved considerable levels of development. In the last 25 years, 650 sites have been excavated, including the ruins of nearby pyramids, measuring 20 m (66 ft) in height, and large abandoned settlements. Regardless, the civilisation continues to be identified by its unique and enigmatic legacy.

Bird's eye view

The greatest mystery of these geoglyphs is that they can only be seen in their full glory from the air when flying over the desert.

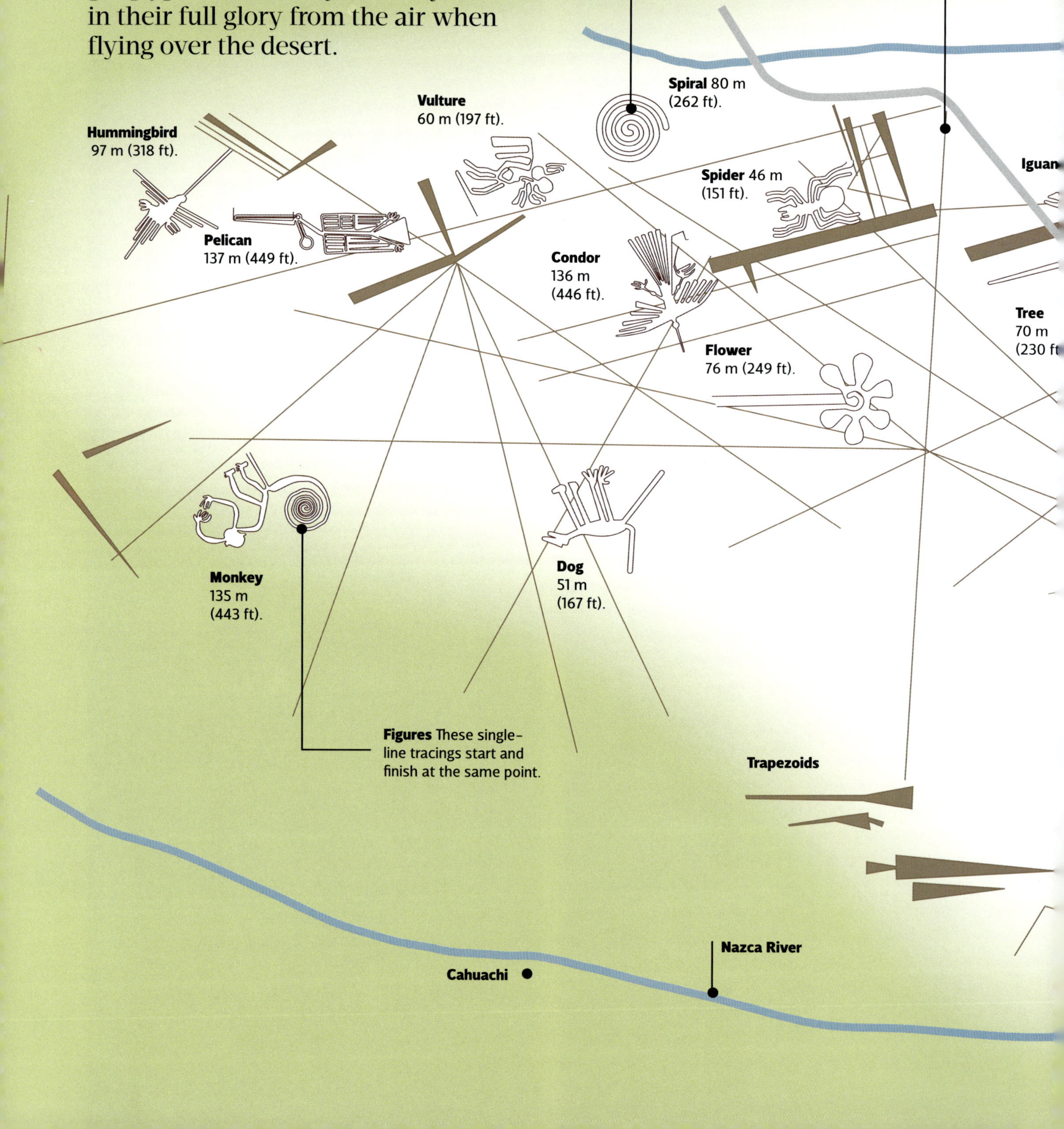

Avenues The avenues have a rectangular, triangular or trapezoidal shape. The lines are astonishingly straight despite measuring hundreds of metres and, in some cases, crossing obstacles such as hills and ravines.

Pan-American Highway Its construction divided some drawings in half, such as the giant lizard.

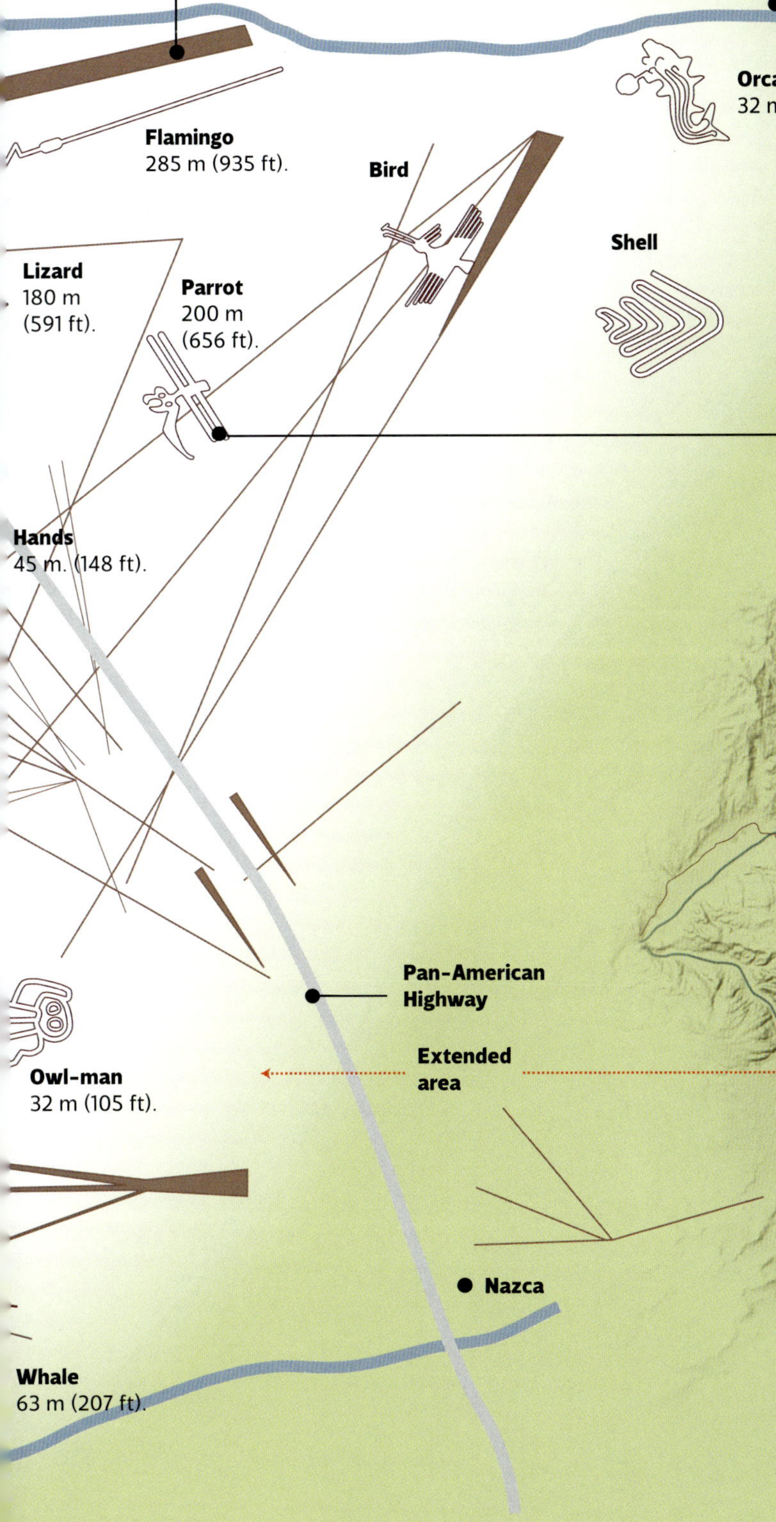

Birds The most commonly featured zoomorphic figures. The flamingo is the largest of them all, measuring 300 m (984 ft) in length.

Size The lines extend over a total area of 450 km^2 (174 mi^2), between Palpa and Nazca provinces, mostly in the pampa of Jumana.

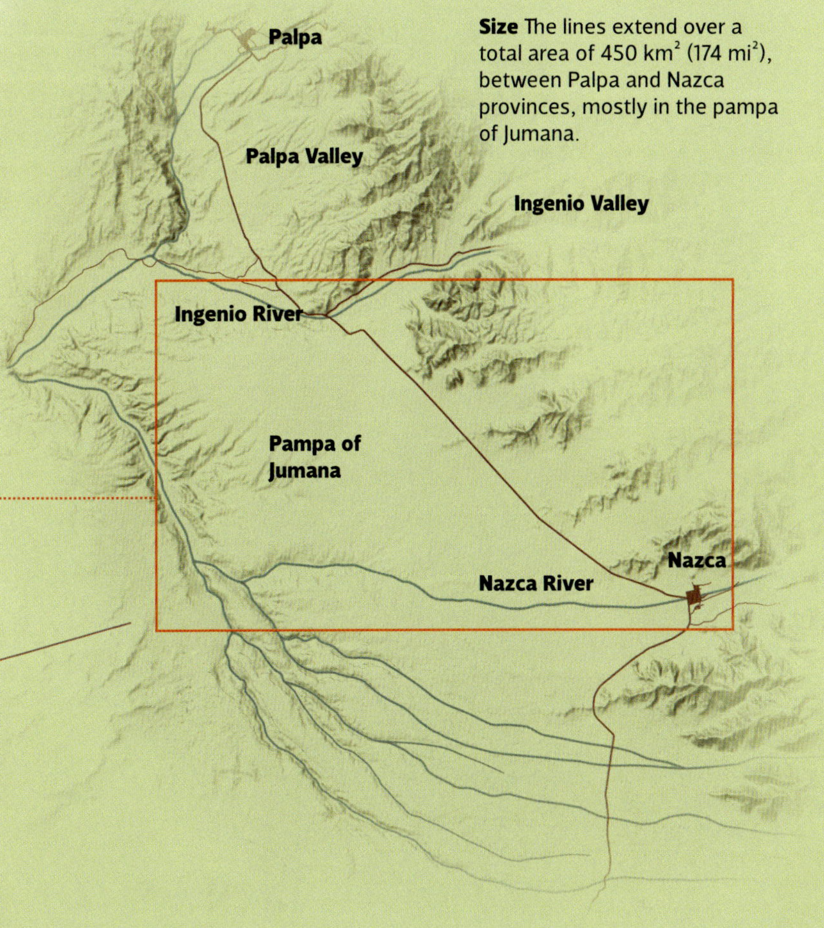

CHICHEN ITZÁ

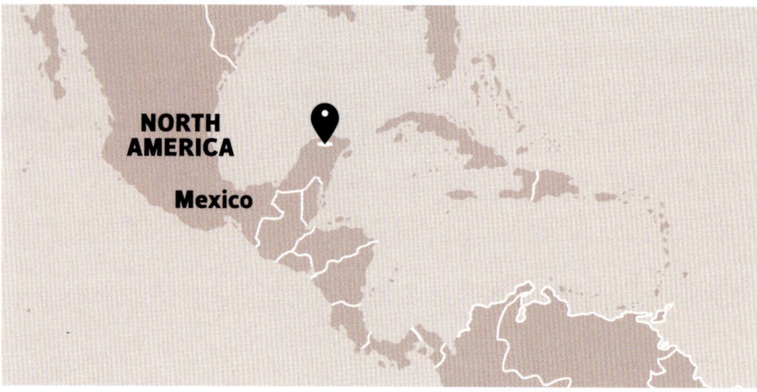

Chichen Itzá Located on the Yucatan Peninsula, 120 km (75 mi) from Merida, in Mexico, Chichen Itzá is one of the most important remaining archaeological sites of the Mayan civilisation.

The great Mayan city

The ruins of Chichen Itzá represent the most impressive assembly of Mayan buildings in the Yucatan. They are a testament to the incredible knowledge of this Mesoamerican civilisation.

The Yucatan Peninsula, which juts into the Gulf of Mexico, separating it from the Caribbean, is a privileged region that houses the most important architectural and cultural treasures of the Mayan civilisation. The ruins at Chichen Itzá are the greatest example of the area's Mayan heritage. Although the city, the name of which translates as the well-head of the water magicians, was founded in the first decades of the 6th century, its period of greatest development and splendour was between the 10th and 16th centuries. It was during this period that almost all the monuments that can be seen at the archaeological site of some 3 km^2 (1.1 mi^2), and that have survived until the present day, were built: monuments documented as authentic masterpieces of Mesoamerican architecture, with influences from the two main cultures: Puuc, of Mayan tradition and Toltec, of the Mexican high plateau. The refinement of the construction, and the delicate decorations carved as a testament to the civilisation's rich mythology have exerted a cultural influence that can still be felt to this day.

During the first half of the life of Chichen Itzá, the darkest in its history, other buildings such as Las Monjas temple, the House of the Deer and the Temple of the Panels, all of which served a ritual purpose, were built. Also dating back to this period, the cenotes, or pools from which underground water was extracted, were also used to perform ritual offerings. By the end of the 9th century, the city had become an important political-religious site of the Mayab (as the Yucatan was known to the Mayans), taking precedence over other important cities such as Balam, Izamal, T'Ho and Champotón. However, it was not until the 10th century that it became the power hub on the peninsula. The shift was not a coincidence, taking place at the same time as the Tolteca invasion and the merging of the two cultures.

It was during this period that the Kukulkan (the Pyramid of the Feathered Serpent), was built, one of the most famous Mayan buildings. Each of its four faces has 91 steps, and counting the platform on top as the final step, they add up to 365, one for every day of the year. This mathematical

↑Reliefs They represent Mayan deities, warriors of different military orders and totem animals.

↗Steps The steps of the pyramids are very steep and narrow.

and astronomical precision, demonstrating the high level of scientific knowledge of the city's priestly class, is present in every detail of each Mayan building at Chichen Itzá. Here, there are no coincidences or mere decorations; everything serves a ceremonial purpose, and has been designed based on astral calculations. The orientation of the structure is so precise that it allows the shadows of some carved decorations to be projected on to the pyramid's steps, creating the illusion of a feathered serpent that descends towards the base. This visual phenomenon was a sign that priests used as motivation to call locals to agricultural work, announcing the arrival of the rainy season and the start of the planting season (with corn being the staple crop).

The Caracol, a circular building that served as an astronomical observatory, was built on a large rectangular platform, 67 m (220 ft) from north to south, 52 m (171 ft) east to west, and 6 m (20 ft) in height. Above this base, a cylindrical tower measuring 16 m (52 ft) in height was erected. It has two spiral-shaped interior and circular galleries, and a small arched chamber that was used as an observatory. While its name is due to the circular steps that communicated its rooms, it is a testament to the advanced and sophisticated calculation and calendar system used by the Mayans. Perhaps the most transcendent factor in assessing this system is the understanding of the concept of zero, the sign of which was represented by the shape of a shell. This was done to prevent confusion with figures made up of dots and lines, combined to express numerical values. Mathematics and their accuracy also played their part in ball games, with the Great Ball Court still visible to this day, around 150 m (492 ft) from Kukulkan pyramid. There, locals would meet to play the Mayan ball game that required significant skill and coordination, playing with their hips

↑The feathered serpent This symbolises the Mayan god Kukulkan and can be seen in many of the columns and lintels of the archaeological complex.

↗The Ball Game The largest pitch in Mesoamerica, measuring 166 m (545 ft) long and 68 m (223 ft) wide. Players had to pass the ball through these rings, located 7.5 m (25 ft) above ground.

↑Palace of the Thousand Columns It is believed that these columns supported a roof, and that the space was used as a meeting area.

or stones as racquets; the game would usually culminate in a ritual offering. The exuberance of constructions, such as the Temple of Warriors and the Palace of the Thousand Columns, are an architectural feature unique to Chichen Itzá, as these types of cylindrical columns were not typical of Mesoamerican buildings. Constructions were designed to satisfy the conquering and aggressive impulses that characterised the region, seen in the growing militarisation of society, around the 11th and 12th centuries; this period also coincided with the arrival of the Tolteca people. At the monument known as Skull Platform, the heads of hundreds of enemies were staked as displayed sacrifices.

The arrivals of the Spanish in the Yucatan, at the beginning of the 16th century, allowed two explorers, Francisco de Montejo and Diego de Landa, to witness the existence of the then abandoned city. However, the first archaeological research did not take place until the middle of the 19th century. And since then, and following looting of the site, this wonder of Mayan civilisation has been recovered.

Kukulkan pyramid

At 24 m (79 ft) high and 55 m (180 ft) wide, this stepped pyramid is the most famous construction at Chichen Itzá.

The feathered serpent At the entrance to the temple there are two serpent-shaped columns, associated with the god Kukulkan, creator of the universe.

Stepped faces The pyramid has four stepped faces, each with 91 steps in total. The northern face is the only one to have two serpent heads at its base. On two days every year, 21 March and 21 September, the shadow that is projected on to the steps takes on the form of a snake.

Inside the pyramid There is another structure measuring 16 m (52 ft) in height. It is believed that the current pyramid was built around the structure, which dates back to the 9th century.

The temple It served a religious purpose, most probably to worship Kukulkan. It features carved wood and a vaulted Mayan ceiling, encompassed by a narrow corridor.
Levels It comprises nine platforms separated in the middle by each of the stepped faces.

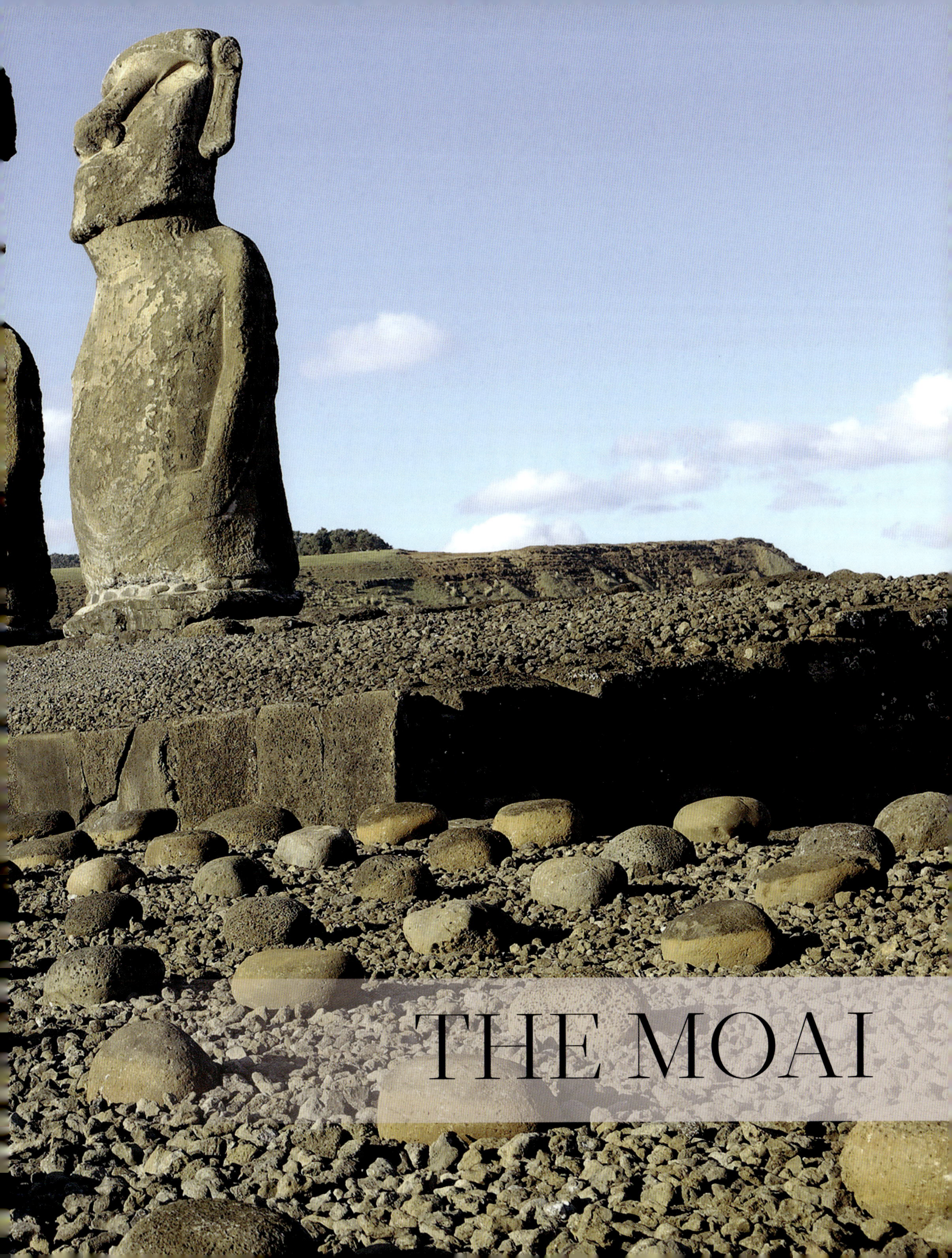

THE MOAI

Easter Island Also known as Rapa Nui, this Chilean island is located in Polynesia, in a remote part of the Pacific Ocean. It measures 163.6 km^2 (63 mi^2) and has around 5,000 inhabitants.

A monumental mystery

The colossal stone statues that are a feature of every corner of Easter Island are a unique cultural phenomenon. Their size is impressive, whilst the mystery in which they are shrouded is somewhat disturbing.

Primitive, huge and sculpted using a significant amount of imagination over a thousand years ago, the moai, as they are known indigenously, are a unique wonder of Easter Island, or Rapa Nui, as it is called in the island's native language. Located in the South Pacific, the island is over 3,500 km (2,175 m) from the South American coast.

Rapa Nui is a synonym for mystery, generated by the spectacular and enigmatic statues. It is also known as Te Pito o Te Henua (Navel of the World) and Mata ki te rangi (Eyes that look to the sky). It is believed that the island was populated by Polynesians that arrived throughout the 4th century, apparently having set sail from the Marquesas Islands. The primitive character of the society evolved into a deeply spiritual and religious culture, tightly bound to nature, that started to sculpt these great statues in around the 10th century. The monuments are even more impressive considering that they were sculpted without the help of machinery or advanced tools to move the rocks that weigh, in some cases, between 50 and 80 tonnes.

Today, the moai are a world-renowned attraction that bring thousands of tourists and researchers to the island. The amount of research carried out on Easter Island at the turn of the 21st century was unprecedented for this Polynesian island; some of the resulting conclusions have facilitated a greater understanding of how the statues were created. The Rapanui extracted blocks of basalt rock or tuff from the immense central peak of the Rano Raraku volcano, located one kilometre from the coastline to the east of the island; they were then sculpted and transported to pre-designated sites. The methods that were used to transport the blocks are still unknown. Some archaeologists support the idea that they were moved by groups of men with ropes that rolled the blocks to their final destination. Others have speculated about the possible use of sleds or wooden wheels; however, this is pure conjecture. Some research completed after the turn of the century has even suggested the possibility that they used complex machines that used a high level of engineering to pull the monumental stones up the slopes of the island.

↑Ko Te Riku Restored in 1974, this is the only Moai on the island that has painted eyes. A disturbing gaze emanates from its face.

Another of the island's mysteries – the purpose of the moai – is still to be solved. The most commonly accepted theory, accepted even by descendants of the Rapanui, is that the statues served a ritual purpose, in memory of the islanders' ancestors. Thus, the statues were distributed around the perimeter of the island, always looking inwards and with their backs to the sea. This was a way of projecting their mana (a supernatural protective power) on the deceased's descendants. Therefore, they were positioned on ahus, ceremonial sloped pedestals. Currently, the fullest and most commonly visited ahu, amongst the 300 on the island, is Tongariki, with 15 aligned moai of varying sizes. Originally, the cavities that represented the eyes of the statues were filled with coral or red volcanic rock, in the belief that this bestowed a soul upon the rock and converted it into an aringa ora: a living face. The monoliths were carefully sculpted in a similar style, in which large noses and long ears predominate. Perhaps the most interesting feature is the headdress that can still be seen on some of the figures; a type of red stone in the form of a circle which was placed on their head once the moai had been erected.

Between the 10th and 17th centuries, around 700 moai were sculpted and placed in position around the perimeter of the 163 km^2 (63 mi^2) island. Furthermore, almost 400 more half-finished sculptures were found later in the volcanic quarry itself. The constant development of the Rapanui resulted in crisis and social upheaval on the island. The definitive break-up took place during the 16th century, with a dispute between the two groups on the island: the Long Ears and the Short Ears. This conflict had a serious impact on Rapanui society and caused the overturning and destruction of many of the moai, in the form of retaliation. This was how the first European visitor, Dutchman Jakob Roggeven, found the island in 1722. During the 20th century, many

↑Arms and hands The majority of moai have arms stuck to their torso and hands with very long fingers.

↗Buried A number of moai have been found partially buried underground.

↗Rano Raraku It is believed that the stone blocks used to create the moai were removed from the crater of this volcano.

→Pukao A stone circle that crowned a number of moai as a hat or headdress.

↑Tongariki This is the largest assembly of moai on the island, with 15 aligned statues.

of the moai were restored and re-erected. Furthermore, just a few years ago, a number of moai that were previously partially buried, with only their heads visible on the surface, were dug out. Groups of archaeologists even discovered inscriptions on the body of the rock that are still to be deciphered.

The enigma of the Rapanui is still alive and is a continuing source of conflict. Norwegian adventurer Thor Heyerdahl maintained that the influence of pre-Columbian cultures in South America was important in the development and mythology of the island. Heyerdal crossed the Pacific in 1947, in the balsa wood raft named 'Kon-Tiki', in an attempt to demonstrate that indigenous South American civilisations could have influenced the conquest of Polynesia. His theories are upheld today by French archaeologist Jean Hervé Daude, who maintains that the two groups that formed Rapanui society clashed in an ethnic dispute: the Short Ears, of Polynesian origin against the Long Ears, of Incan origin. Yet another mystery to add to the origin of the moai.

The arrival of the Rapanui

There are somewhere around 700 moai statues spread around the whole island: the principal traces left by the original population.

Ahus 288 moai are associated with the ahus, with the remainder spread across the island.

Maunga Terevaka 506 m (1,660 ft).

Distribution The majority of moai are positioned on the coast; however, around twenty are positioned inland.

Hanga Roa The capital and only settlement on the island.

Rano Kau 324 m (1,063 ft).

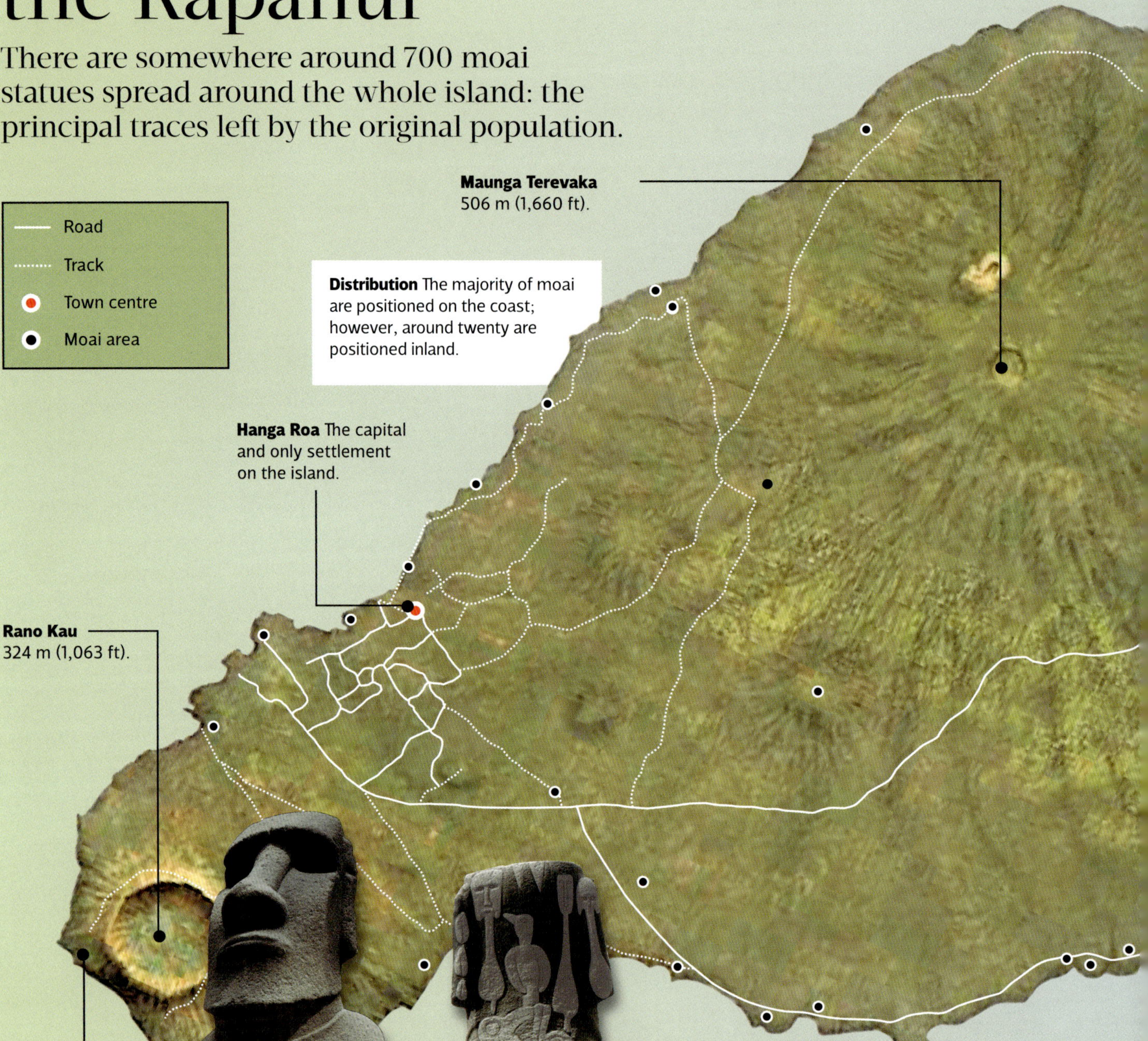

Orongo Ceremonial centre.

Hoa Hakananai'a This unique moai was found in a house at the Orongo ceremonial centre. Today, it can be visited in the British Museum. It weighs four tonnes and measures 2.5 m (8 ft) in height. Similar to other moai, it had a sculpted torso; however, it is particularly noteworthy due to the figures linked to the Bird Man cult.

Pukao 58 of the moai wear this red rock headdress, the average weight of which is 10 tonnes.

Material Sculpted from volcanic rock, mostly tuff, although a dozen were sculpted from basalt.

Eyes Made from coral or obsidian and, in some cases, painted. All have been restored, as when the statues were discovered, the inlays that represented the eyes of the moai had been lost.

Rano Raraku volcano 100 m (328 ft). Its outer slopes and crater were where the moai were sculpted.

Ahu Tongariki The largest ahu on the island, made up of 15 moai.

ANGKOR WAT

Angkor Wat This impressive temple is located in the Siem Riep province in the middle of the Cambodian forest. It forms part of the historic buildings of Angkor.

A forest wonder

It is the largest building in the world built for religious purposes, and the Khmer Empire's masterpiece. Its magnificence has astounded people for a thousand years and continues to amaze all who see it.

Lost amongst the abundant foliage, covered by branches and leaves, the temple appeared suddenly like a wonderful hallucination. Naturalist Henri Mouhot tried, in similar words, to describe the incredible chance find in his book, *Travels in the Central Parts of Indo-China (Siam), Cambodia, and Laos*. The fantastic building, which appeared like something out of a book of oriental magic stories, was discovered in the Cambodian forest in 1860. Mouhot, who died one year later, travelled through south-east Asia in order to carry out scientific research, and, with the posthumous publication of his journals, he became the greatest Western populariser of the existence of this lost palace of Angkor Wat.

Until the eighth century, the interior of present-day Cambodia was a tropical region of dense forest with violent monsoon rains and abundant wildlife. It had neither town nor city. However, after the long war which liberated the Khmers from Javanese invaders, large developments flourished in a very short time. The recovery of their lands led to the period of greatest progress, which ended with the creation of the powerful Khmer Empire at the beginning of the 9th century under Jayavarman II. The monarch's Hindu beliefs led him to build these remarkable temples over a region of some 200 km^2 (77 mi^2) called Angkor. This gave rise to a complex which became the capital of the Empire. The city itself was buzzing with almost half a million people who lived in houses arranged in a grid with wide streets, stores, sanctuaries, several irrigation channels and terraces. Some historians suggest that, at the beginning of the second millennium, it was the largest city in the world for its time.

The expansion of the Khmer Empire increased and, in a couple of centuries, it dominated the lands of Thailand, Laos, Burma and parts of Malaysia in addition to Cambodia. At its peak, at the beginning of the 12th century, King Suryavarnam II, the monarch between 1113 and 1150, ordered the construction of the largest temple of all, dedicated to Vishnu: the palace of Angkor Wat. It was to be the luxurious political and religious nucleus of the Empire and a sacred place used for funerary practices.

↑Aerial view Angkor Wat has three concentric rectangular enclosures which increase in height.

And so it was. Legend has it that, for these reasons, the King wanted to choose a location for the temple which would please the Gods. He released a donkey and let it walk until it sat down: the place where the sacred animal decided to rest is where he built Angkor Wat. At that time, around the area which spans almost 2.6 km^2 (1 mi^2) and is today visited by almost one million tourists every year, more than 20,000 permanent inhabitants lived there as well as the Royal Court. The palace, oriented towards the West, the land of the dead and of the sunset, still retains its four concentric rectangular enclosures. The path leading towards the heart of the palace, where the main building with its 61 m (200 ft) dome is located, measures 305 m (1,000 ft). It is a paved street decorated with reliefs of symbolic scenes which re-create the sacred history of Hinduism. It is a curious detail because, despite being built under the Hindu faith, during the 13th century the Empire switched to the Buddhist faith, although it respected the decoration and Hindu symbolism of the Palace. In reality it created a syncretism, a blending of both religions, which still survives in Khmer descendants today.

Home of the Gods

However, the architectural beauty and wealth, the magnificent terraces, the towers and domes which take the shape of lotus flowers, were built to be observed from the outside, as an offering. The most sacred internal areas did not have big gateways or ceremonial spaces. It was not a meeting place for the faithful, but a resting place for the Gods. Therefore, the site was built to recreate the Hindu universe; its large perimeter lake evokes the surrounding oceans, the enclosures, which increase in height towards the centre, symbolise the slopes and the truncated peak of Mount Meru, the sacred mountain of that region, while the towers represent the different peaks of this legendary mountain.

↑Surrounded by water A large lake 3.6 km (2.2 mi) long and 200 m (656 ft) wide surrounds the temple.

↗Galleries A series of porticoed cloisters connect the second and third enclosure.

↑Apsaras There are some 2,000 dancers from Hindu mythology sculpted into the walls of Angkor Wat.

↗Access A large stone avenue leads to an entrance across the lake.

→Vishnu A huge statue dedicated to the Hindu god located in a portico to the south of the main entrance.

In 1432 the capital was transferred from Angkor to Longvek and Angkor Wat lost its importance, its splendour and fell into disrepair. The same period saw the decline of the Khmers, threatened by Siamese and Mongol raids. Angkor Wat began to forge a new legend, that of the lost city, although it is certain that the large palace was partially occupied during the 16th century and that the Buddhist monks never abandoned it completely.

Henri Mouhot's publications led to the creation of the École Française d'Extrême-Orient (French School of the Far East), in 1898, in order to study and preserve the treasures of Indo-China artistic heritage, under French protection. For over a hundred years, interrupted in the 1970s by the brutal dictatorship of the Khmer Rouge, Angkor Wat has been in a state of permanent restoration. The mould and lichens have been cleaned from the stones and the giant sculpted faces and many of the collapsed sections have been rebuilt. And although neither the polychrome nor the magnificent wooden roofs can be recovered, the former splendour has returned displaying its imposing symbolic power.

Political and religious centre

Hidden by the forest for centuries and today a tourist attraction, the temple of Angkor Wat was the political and religious centre of the Khmer Empire.

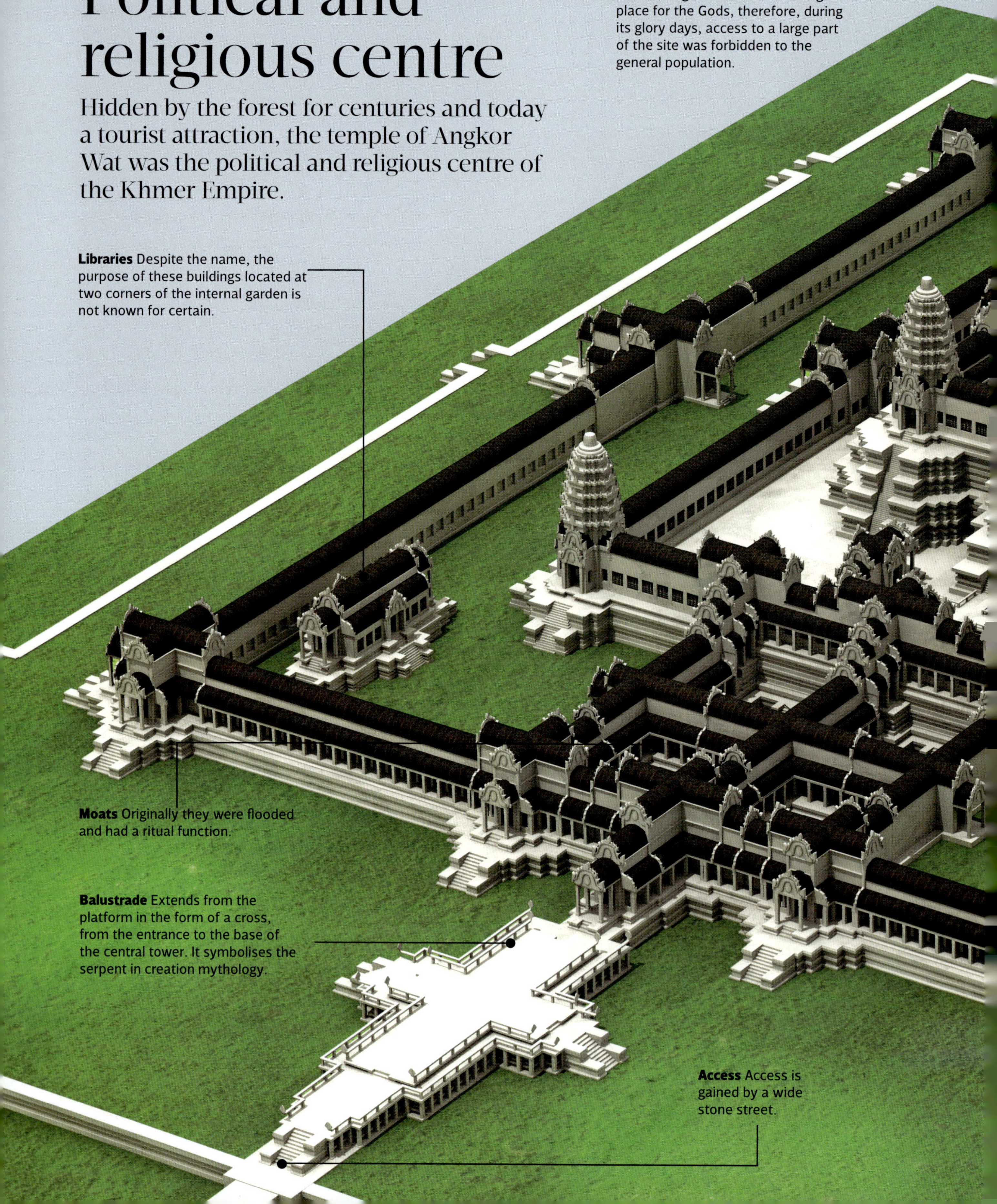

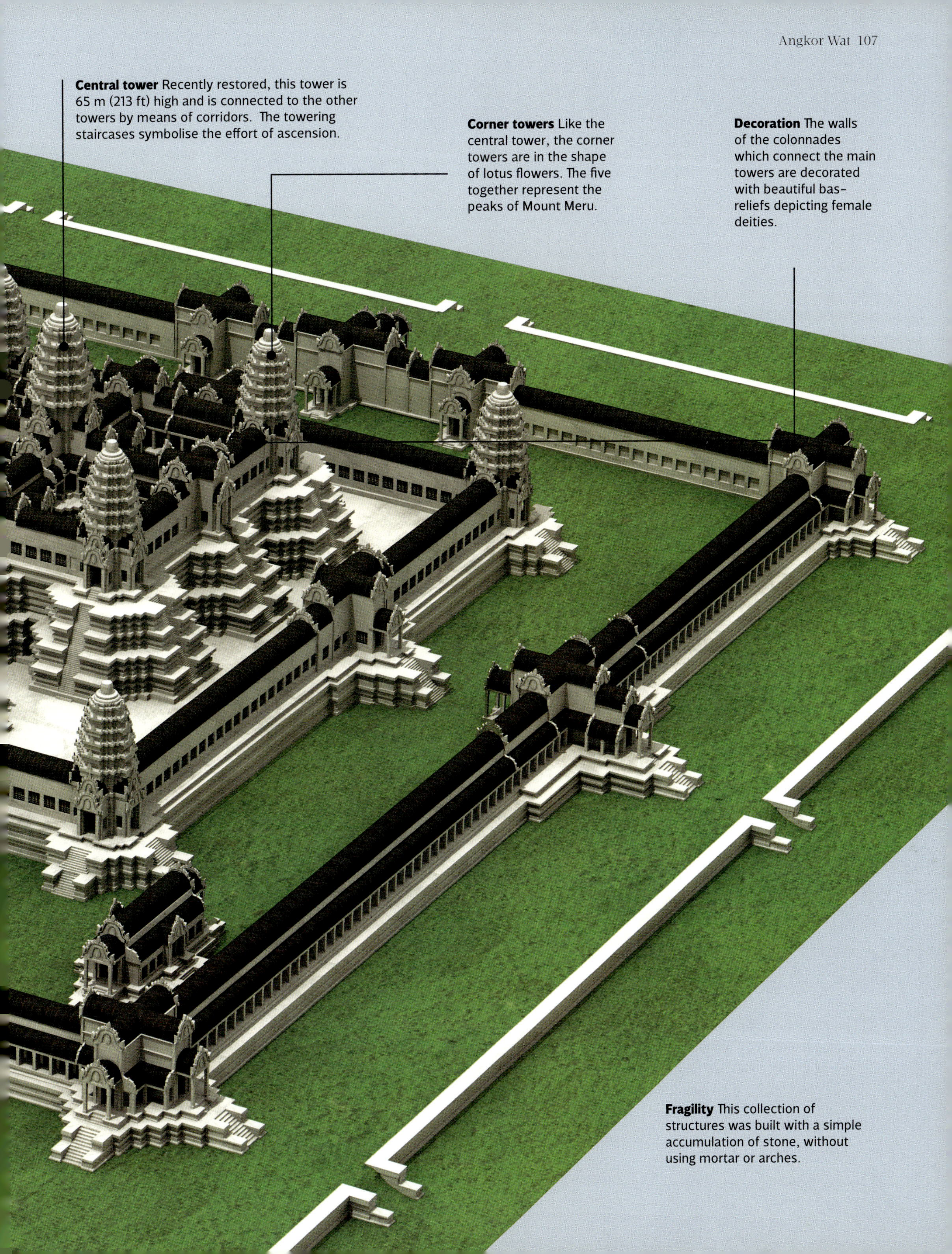
Central tower Recently restored, this tower is 65 m (213 ft) high and is connected to the other towers by means of corridors. The towering staircases symbolise the effort of ascension.
Corner towers Like the central tower, the corner towers are in the shape of lotus flowers. The five together represent the peaks of Mount Meru.
Decoration The walls of the colonnades which connect the main towers are decorated with beautiful bas-reliefs depicting female deities.
Fragility This collection of structures was built with a simple accumulation of stone, without using mortar or arches.

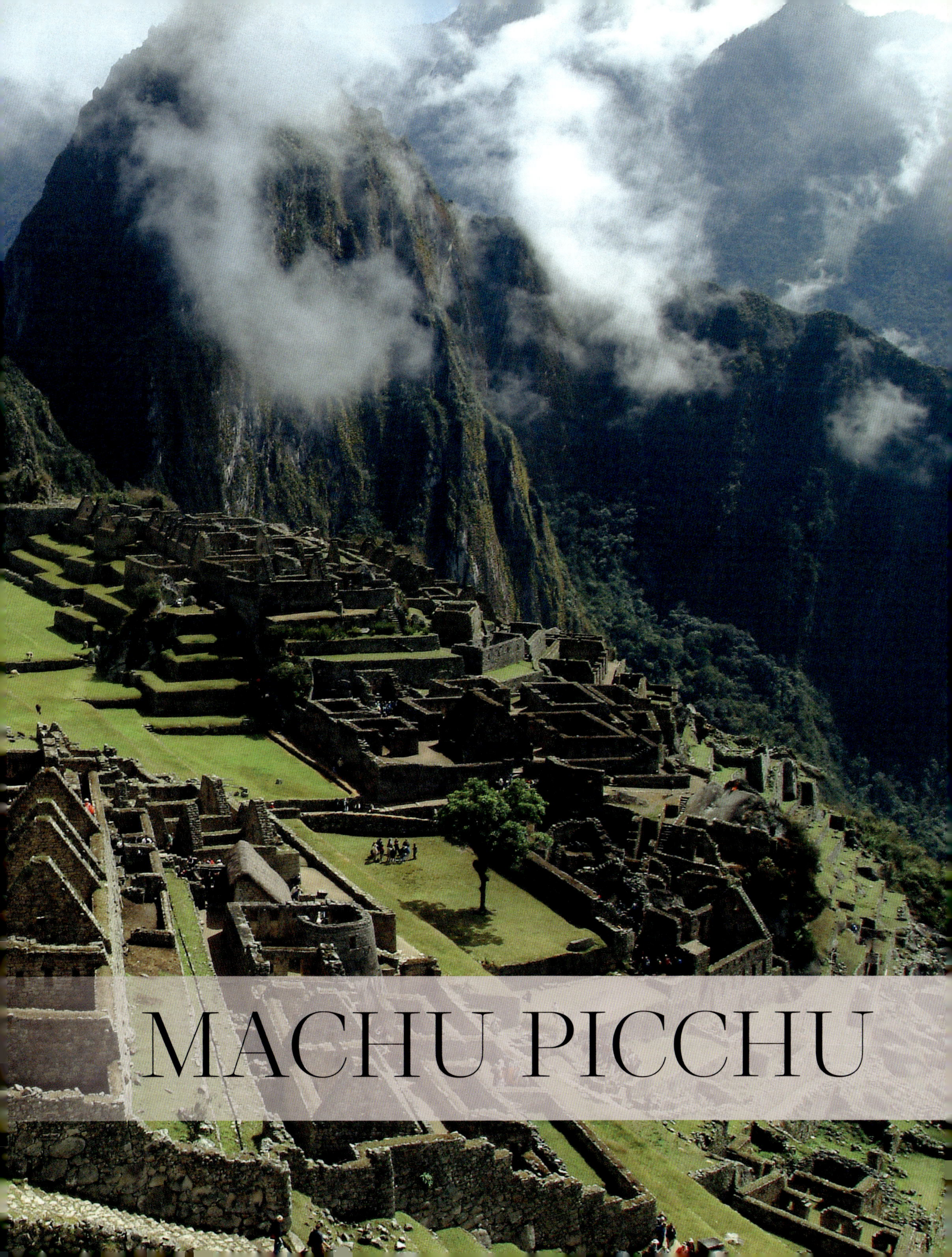

MACHU PICCHU

Machu Picchu This most impressive Inca city is located at an altitude of 2,400 m (7,874 ft) in the Peruvian Andes, in the south of the country.

The secret of the Incas

Enveloped in the Andean mountain mists, the abandoned city of the Incas still exudes an aura of mystery and respect for this civilisation.

This sacred and inaccessible citadel was the jewel of Incan urban architecture. Its walls, slopes and cultivated terraces were designed with the greatest constructive ingenuity, not only in terms of getting around the problem of the rugged terrain, but also in adapting the forms and size of its buildings to the surrounding natural environment so it appears to be carved from the stone of the mountain.

In the heart of Peru, more than 2,400 m (7,874 ft) high where the mountains of the Andes are inaccessible, and more than 80 km (49 mi) north-east of Cuzco, Machu Picchu, the former capital of the Incan Empire, remained hidden for more than 300 years; quite the opposite of today's situation. Its terraces, covered with bright green vegetation, and its walls and palaces rebuilt during the last century, are visited by almost 2,000 tourists daily. According to experts, this number is too high and is affecting the city's conservation. Visitors' footprints erode the stones of the Inca trail leading to the citadel, bringing with them the risk of collapse.

It wasn't always like this. 'For centuries it was impossible for travellers to access the site because a steep granite precipice rising 600 m (2,000 ft) from the banks of the river defied any effort made to overcome it. The peasants who cultivated cocoa and sugar in the low valleys of the Urubamba could only carry their products to market by crossing a snowy pass of almost 4,300 m (14,108 ft). Later they persuaded the Peruvian government to open up a pathway by drilling into the granite cliff-face, unaware that a large Inca sanctuary was hidden in the upper part of the canyon'. As American history professor Hiram Bingham explains, this is the reason that Machu Picchu remained forgotten for such a long time until an expedition, which he led, found it on the 20 July 1911.

A different version states that, nine years before, Peruvian landowner Miguel Lizárraga had already arrived at the so-called 'Lost City of the Incas', on the 14 July 1902. However, Machu Picchu was not a lost city in the strictest sense; even Bingham supported this idea, because there were always peasants working in the

↑A city in the clouds A large part of Machu Picchu's charm is its beautiful and majestic location.

surrounding valleys despite the resident population having moved on. Instead, it is possible to talk about a city, not conquered, not occupied, but one whose peak lasted for one hundred years.

Example of precision and ingenuity

The first Inca, Pachacútec, ordered it to be built around 1450, when Tawantinsuyu (Incan Empire territory) reached its furthest point, from the south of Columbia to the north of Chile and Argentina. There, in the crest of two mountains, Machu Picchu and Huayna Picchu, the Emperor stood amazed by the sight of the natural surroundings: the grandeur of the mountains, the unsettling view of the sheer drop into the deep canyon and the turbulent channel of water caused by the bends in the sacred river Urubamba. He built the city there in a great show of ingenuity. The steepest region some 500 m (1,640 ft) long by 200 m (656 ft) wide was utilised to bunch together more than 170 enclosures, ranging from properties to religious temples, while the steepest part of the southern slope was dedicated to farmed terraces.

One of the greatest construction secrets is how the buildings are supported in a region which is geologically unstable and where landslides caused by the heavy rains are commonplace. The Incan architects devised a drainage system for the exposed areas, with layers of gravel and rock which filtered the water and prevented soil erosion. The system had 129 drainage channels which led rainwater to the city drain in the southern section exactly where the farmed terraces were located. This not only prevented erosion of the soil but also facilitated irrigation. As with other, particularly older cities of Andean cultures, such as Tiwanaku, the religious tradition dictated the design of the buildings in terms of orientation and positioning, respecting the transit of the sun during

↑The dwellings Detail showing one of the houses built with stone and cemented with a mud mortar.

↗Terraces This system enabled the Incas to cultivate crops on the steep slopes of the mountain.

→Urban development A wonder of perfect planning and architecture, structured over different urban areas.

↑Royal tomb The tomb was dug from solid rock and has detailed engravings.

the summer solstice. The urban citadel was divided into two large sections: the Hanan or upper part, where the royal and sacred buildings are located (Temple of the Sun, Inca Palace, Sacred Square) and the Hurin where dwellings and areas allocated for work and provisions (water sources, quarries, workshops and female residences) are found.

The Spanish Conquistadors, who didn't arrive in the region until 1570, never occupied it, although they imposed taxes on the valley's inhabitants and peasants. Machu Picchu always commands ancestral respect owing to its location and its image of a city suspended in the clouds. But as time went by it was abandoned, although, looters and plunderers continued to visit the site. Even Professor Bingham transferred more than 46,300 items, which he had discovered during three years excavating the Incan city to Yale University, in the United States of America. Since 2008 however, the American University has begun to restore this material following petitions made by the Peruvian government.

A display of Incan ingenuity

The city of Machu Picchu has clearly defined agricultural areas as well as designated urban areas where temples and properties are located.

Distribution The city is divided into two sections, one farming and the other urban, separated by a staircase, a wall and a ditch which also serves as a drainage channel.

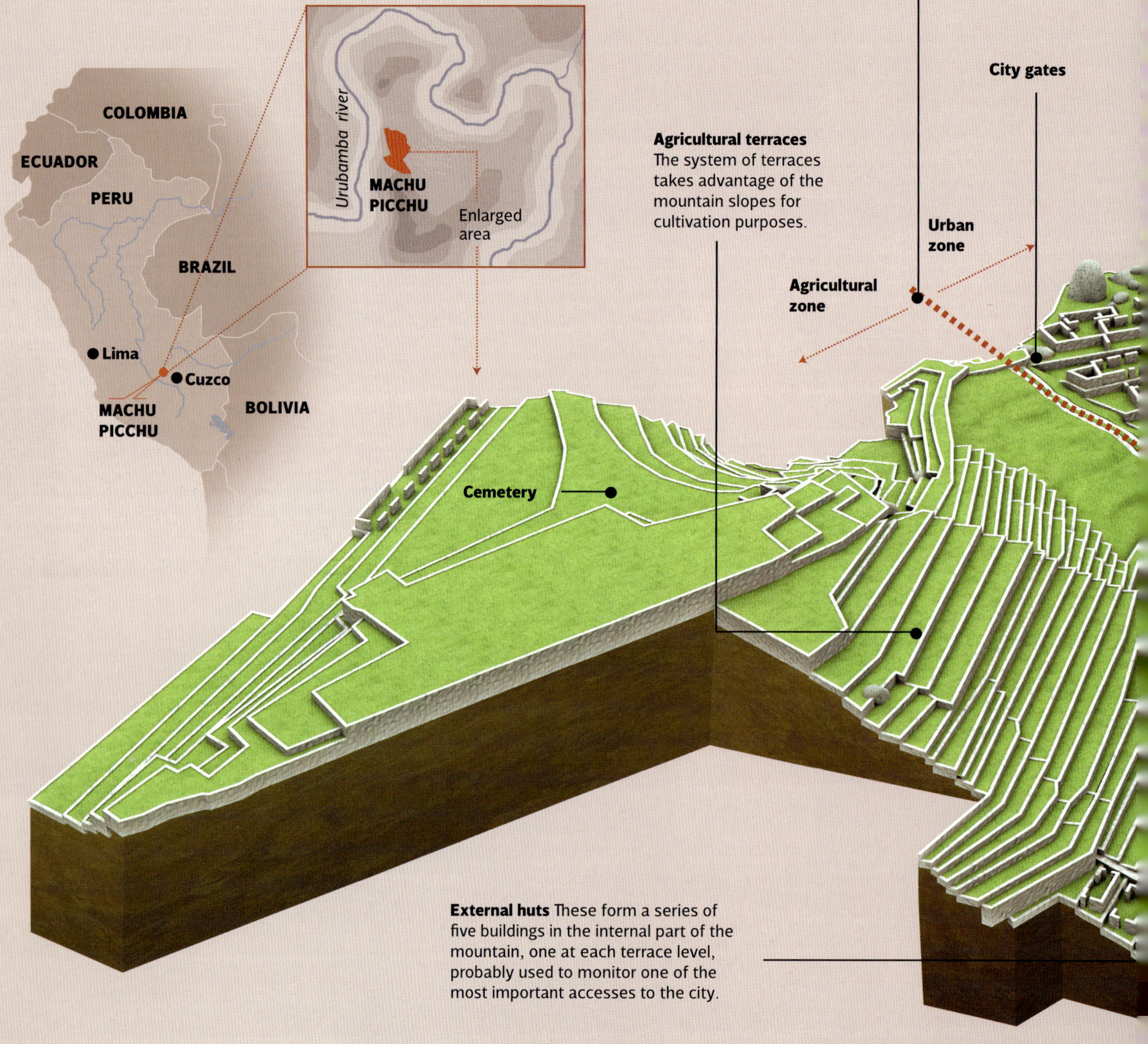

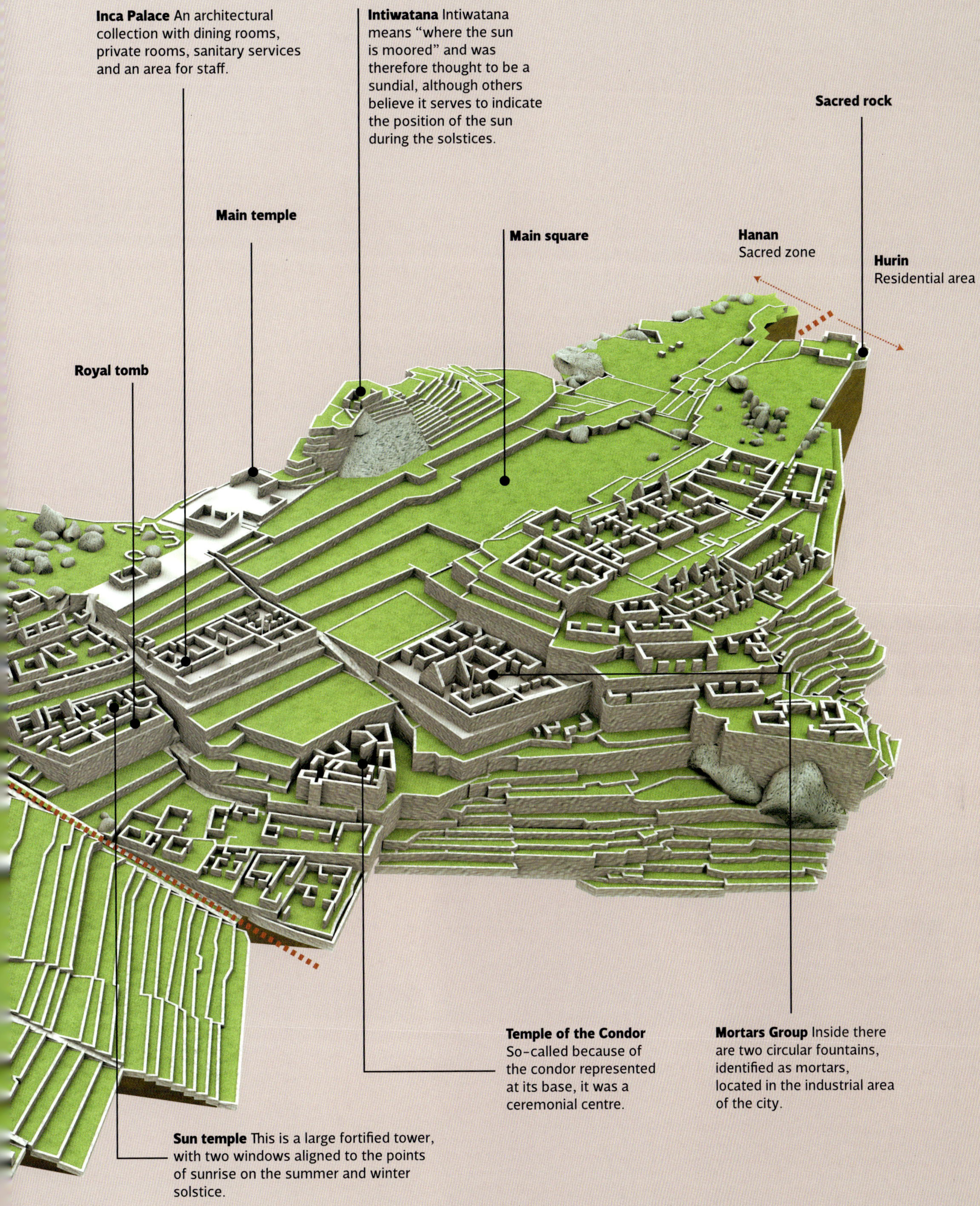
Inca Palace An architectural collection with dining rooms, private rooms, sanitary services and an area for staff.
Intiwatana Intiwatana means "where the sun is moored" and was therefore thought to be a sundial, although others believe it serves to indicate the position of the sun during the solstices.
Sacred rock
Main temple
Main square
Hanan
Sacred zone
Hurin
Residential area
Royal tomb
Temple of the Condor So-called because of the condor represented at its base, it was a ceremonial centre.
Mortars Group Inside there are two circular fountains, identified as mortars, located in the industrial area of the city.
Sun temple This is a large fortified tower, with two windows aligned to the points of sunrise on the summer and winter solstice.

太和殿

FORBIDDEN CITY

Beijing This palatial enclosure covers 720,000 m^2 (7,750,080 ft^2) in the heart of Beijing, the capital of China.

Imperial privilege

The Imperial enclosure of the Forbidden City, in the heart of Beijing, the capital of China, is an artistic, architectural and symbolic wonder which far exceeds the imagination of any observer.

The mysterious Forbidden City, a sacred stronghold for the last two dynasties of the Chinese Empire, is now an open space which shows the world the splendour that for 500 years was reserved exclusively for the Imperial elite. It's not strictly a city, it is a large palatial enclosure, and the largest built in wood in the world. Its full name is The Purple Forbidden City, in response to the Chinese translation Tse-kin-ch'eng which refers to the polar star as the centre of the sky, a symbolism which, for the Chinese, is reflected in the fact that these imperial palaces were the centre of the Earth. It was rightly called forbidden because it could only be entered or exited with the express permission of the Emperor.

It covers an area of 720,000 m^2 (7,750,015 ft^2), measuring some 960 m (3,150 ft) north to south and 750 m (2,461 ft) east to west, and is surrounded by a moat and walls more than 8 m (26 ft) high. Work began on this massive project in 1406. It took around half a million workers 15 years to build the complex which was completed in 1420. It was carried out under the orders of Yong Lu, the third Ming Dynasty Emperor. After being the residence of 24 emperors, 14 from the Ming dynasty and 10 from the Qing dynasty, in 1912, the Forbidden City ceased to be the political centre of China after the abdication of Puyi, the last Emperor of the Qing dynasties and of the former Chinese regime. In the 500 years of Imperial development, the Forbidden City suffered invasions, partial destruction and fire over different periods but it was always rebuilt and the symbolic power and design essentially never changed. Of the four gates on the site, the Midday Gate (Wumen) is the main and largest gate. It has a large central corridor and four pavilions that extend beyond the terraces of the city walls. Behind the large gate there are 980 buildings in the city, although only one part can be visited today.

Although the Forbidden City is now a large museum, the north-south axis continues to serve as the backbone of the palatial enclosure just as it did during the period of imperial splendour. It has a marble avenue, a passage which only the Emperor could travel along carried in his

↑Throne room The three halls of Harmony have a richly decorated throne room.

sedan chair. The path links the Midday Gate, to the north, with the Gateway of Heavenly Peace to the south and is bordered by sculptures of dragons and clouds.

In the centre of the city, and on its axis, the Harmony collection of buildings can be found, directly linked to the life and activities of the Emperor. The Hall of Supreme Harmony, one of the largest buildings made of wood in China, is the site of great ceremonies held during Chinese New Year celebrations, as well as winter solstice celebrations and the Emperor's anniversary. The Imperial throne of the Dragon Throne, decorated in gold lacquer, can still be seen today in the centre of this palace. Along the same symbolic line is the Hall of Complete Harmony (Chung Ho Tien) and the Hall of Preserving Harmony (Pao Ho Tien); the latter with its five naves was the Emperor's reception hall where he received men of high intellectual status. The Palace of Heavenly Purity (Tsien Tsing Kong), the private residence of the Emperor, is located in the internal courtyard. But his rooms were located in the Palace of Exquisite Heart (Yang Sin Tien), located on the western side of the internal courtyard. All these buildings were built in the same way and in the same style: plinths and stone bases upon which a wooden structure was erected with gently curving roofs covered with yellow tiles, the Imperial colour. The rest of the palaces and pavilions, together with the terraces, were allocated to the empress, the Imperial concubines and the official residences.

A great art collection

Today, the site is administered by an official body, the Palace Museum, which is carrying out a restoration project to restore all the buildings and return them to their condition prior to 1912. In addition, it is classifying all objects being exhibited and those being conserved.

↑Gate of Supreme Harmony This gateway provides access to the main palaces in front of which is the Golden Water River, crossed by five bridges with marble balustrades.

→Architecture The palaces are made of wood and the roofs are yellow glazed tiles decorated with figures and reliefs.

↑Nine Dragon Wall Built in marble and decorated with ceramic polychrome dragons, it measures 30 m (98 ft) long and 3.5 m (11 ft) high.

The permanent collection comprises approximately one million individual pieces. Although in total and according to a census of the objects carried out over a period of six years (2004–2010), the museum has more than 1,800,000 objects of which around 1,680,000 were classified as priceless cultural relics and are protected by the Chinese state. Amongst these are more than 400 paintings from the 13th and 14th century, from the Yuan dynasties, prior to the Ming dynasties and the construction of the Imperial city. Other artistic gems include 1,600 pieces in bronze dating from the 2nd century BC and 320,000 pieces of porcelain, just from the Imperial collection.

Perhaps one of the most valuable treasures the Forbidden City houses today, greater than its architecture and symbolism, is the collection of jade objects which occupy a special place in Chinese art. It is a collection of 30,000 pieces from the legacy of the Imperial families which goes some way towards understanding the actual extent of artistic depth in this museum, listed as one of the most important in the world.

The palatial complex

The former Imperial residence is now a museum open to the public and receives some seven million visitors each year.

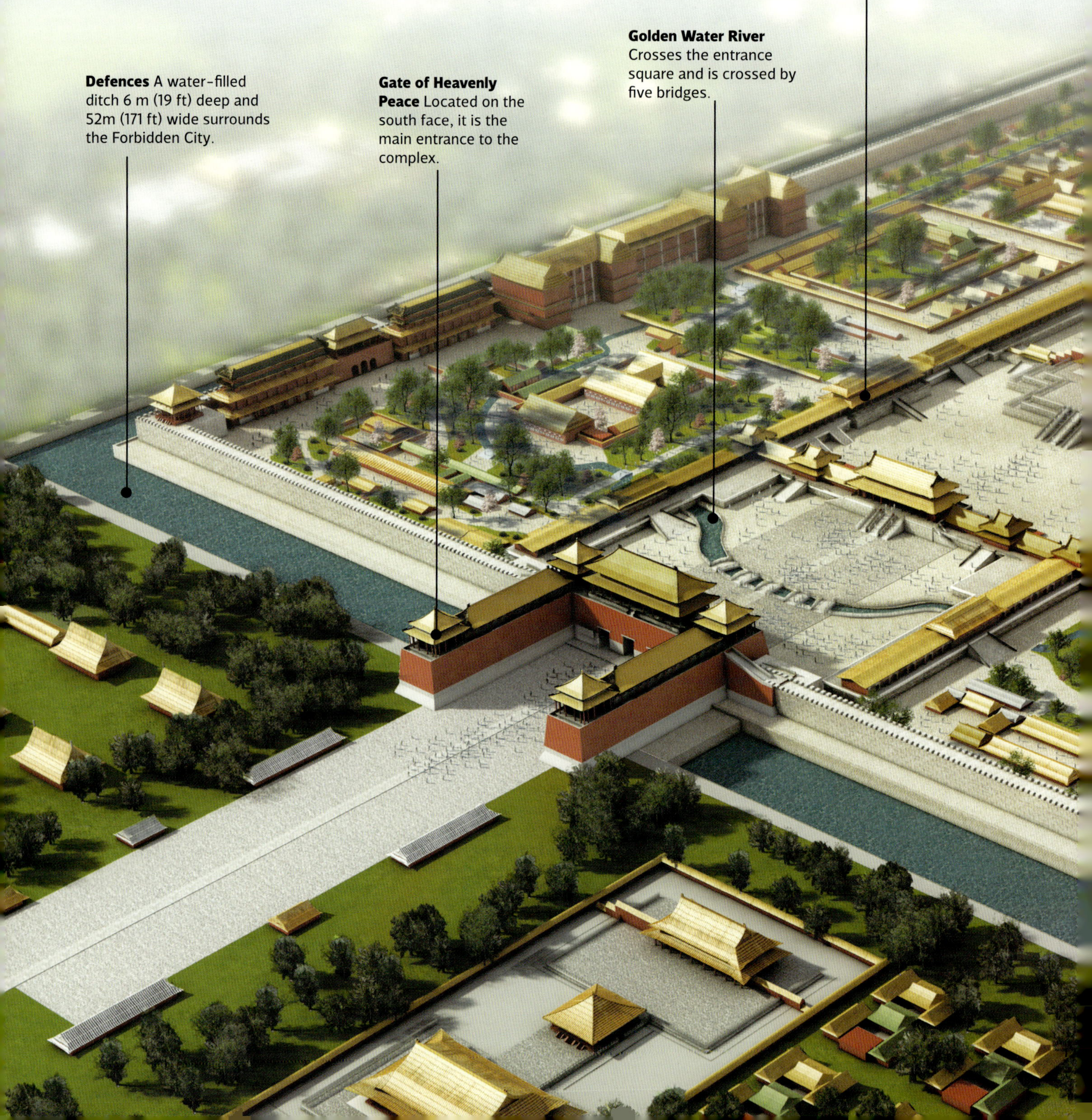

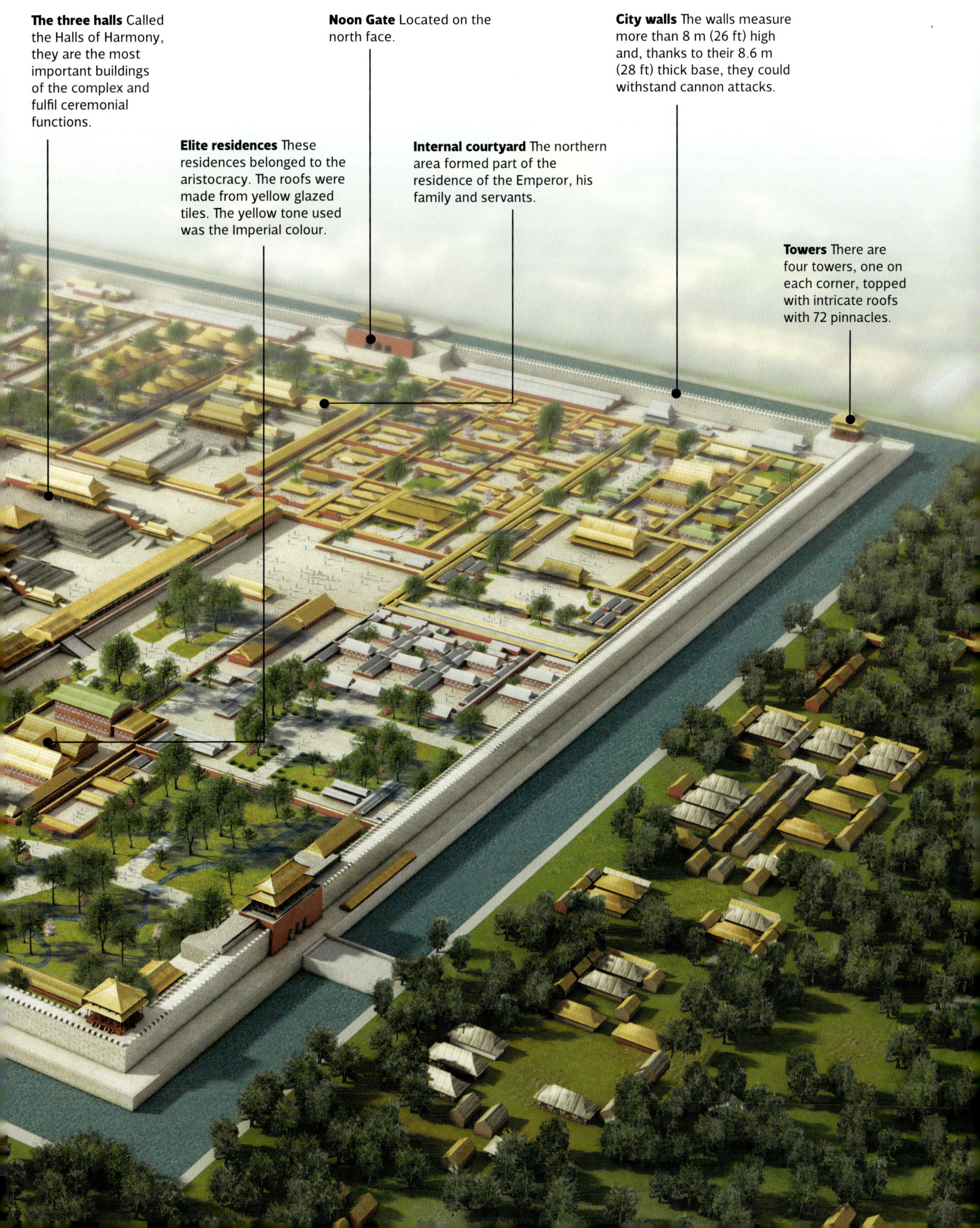
The three halls Called the Halls of Harmony, they are the most important buildings of the complex and fulfil ceremonial functions.
Noon Gate Located on the north face.
City walls The walls measure more than 8 m (26 ft) high and, thanks to their 8.6 m (28 ft) thick base, they could withstand cannon attacks.
Elite residences These residences belonged to the aristocracy. The roofs were made from yellow glazed tiles. The yellow tone used was the Imperial colour.
Internal courtyard The northern area formed part of the residence of the Emperor, his family and servants.
Towers There are four towers, one on each corner, topped with intricate roofs with 72 pinnacles.

HONOREM PRINCIPIS APOST PAVLV
eccetto
atac - taxi

ST PETER'S BASILICA

Rome St Peter's Basilica is located in the Vatican City, a micro state in the city of Rome which covers an area of 0.439 km^2 (0.170 mi^2).

Centre for Christianity

St Peter's Basilica is the largest Christian temple, the residence of the Pope, an artistic treasure, and a building whose spiritual aura exceeds even its significant architectural value.

This unique, almost 500-year-old temple is a living example of Renaissance and Baroque architecture and serves as a fundamental centre for Catholic pilgrimage. Its history however, begins some two millennia ago. Situated outside the historic walls of Rome and to the west of the River Tiber, the then uninhabited region which today is the Vatican State, comprising some 44 hectares, of which only 2.3 belong to the Basilica, was chosen by the Emperor Nero as the site on which to build a circus and a cemetery. In Nero's Circus hundreds of persecuted Christians were executed, among them Peter the apostle, and his remains were buried in the nearby cemetery. Christian tradition states that the place was marked with a rock that was painted red. This symbolised his name, and helped the Christians to identify it. Some 250 years later, the Emperor Constantine, who adopted Christianity as the faith for the Roman Empire, ordered the building of a church exactly on this symbolic site, at the request of Pope Sylvester. However, the spectacular construction which can be seen today began to be developed in the middle of the 15th century when the deterioration and abandonment of the former sanctuary prompted the beginning of construction work to rebuild it, even using stones taken from the partially demolished Colosseum. But it was in the first years of the 16th century when Pope Julius II picked up the idea and proposed a new and ambitious architectural project: the construction of a magnificent building involving the most brilliant architects and artists of the Renaissance period that took over 20 popes and almost 150 years to complete.

Work began on 18 April 1506 under architects Renato Bramante and Giuliano da Sangallo. Years later the site became the responsibility of Rafael Sanzio. Among the numerous professionals who oversaw construction, three in particular stand out: Michelangelo, who designed the dome; Carlo Maderno, who created the facade and the Basilica, and Gian Lorenzo Bernini, whose principal contribution was the magnificent St Peter's Square. The Basilica of today is a compendium of works of art from all genres. Within the enormous structure, which comprises three large naves, 45 altars, 11 chapels and dozens of

↑Harmonious collection View of the dome of the Basilica and St Peter's Square in the shadow of the Egyptian obelisk.

carefully decorated niches and pedestals, are sacred images, paintings representing sacred art, and the tombs of various popes, some in amazing sarcophagi carved into the Basilica, others in the Vatican grottoes. Perhaps one of the best examples of this art is the sublime sculpture by Michelangelo, The Pietà, carved from a single block of marble which he chose from the quarries of the Apuan Alps when he was just 24 years old. It was moved in 1749 and today this artistic gem is displayed in the first chapel to the right of the Basilica's entrance.

A Renaissance wonder

But the work of Michelangelo had its touch of genius in the creation of the immense dome which appears to float above the temple despite being a heavy structure more than 136 m (446 ft) high and with a diameter greater than 41 m (135 ft). Two other magnificent domes inspired Michelangelo in his design: that of the Pantheon also in Rome and the dome of Florence Cathedral. The artist never lived to see his work finished as construction wasn't completed until 1590, some 26 years after his death. Under the dome, in the cross of the basilica, is the chapel altar framed by another of the temple's works of art: a baldachin or canopy, 30 m (98 ft) high, made in bronze with columns imitating those of the legendary Temple of Solomon. This work by Gian Lorenzo Bernini, one of the most famous artists of Italian Baroque, took more than nine years to finish. Directly underneath the marble block which forms the papal altar and is aligned with the centre of the dome, according to tradition, is the location of the original grave of the apostle Peter, marked with a red stone. It is perhaps the site where the spiritual emotion conveyed by the temple reaches a maximum for pilgrims.

Like the baldachin, the main facade was also finished during the first decades of the 17th century. Built under the direction of architect Carlo Maderno, it measures

↑Baldachin This is the work of Bernini. It indicates where the remains of Saint Peter were laid to rest.

↗Dome The internal part is decorated with mosaics by Giuseppe Cesari.

↗The Pietà This work by Michelangelo is the temple's main sculpted jewel.

→Central nave The Basilica has a Latin floor cross with a large central nave 187 m (614 ft) long.

↑Swiss Guard This military body is responsible for protecting the Pope and the Vatican.

115 m (377 ft) wide and stands at a height of 46 m (151 ft). The most important aspects are the great columns that frame the entrances and also the so-called 'Loggia of the Blessings', from where the choice of the new pope is announced and also from where he gives his blessing *Urbi et Orbi* to the faithful.

The Basilica is accessed through five doors: the Door of Death, so-called because it is the exit used for papal funeral processions; the Door of Good and Evil, the Door of the Sacraments, Holy Door and the Filarete Door, the oldest, built before the actual temple in the middle of the 15th century and divided into two magnificent bronze leaves, decorated with panels of images of Christ, the Virgin, St Peter and St Paul. Outside the Basilica, Bernini's master work extends to St Peter's Square where it reaches its maximum splendour in the alignment of the groups of columns which surround it and which have been declared perfect by numerous artists. The square sits in the shadow of the original Egyptian obelisk which decorated Nero's Circus and opposite which the apostle Peter was crucified.

II
VNIT

Architectural perfection

The Basilica and St Peter's Square, devised by Bernini, together make up one of the most beautiful architectural collections in the world.

Michelangelo's dome Measures 42 m (138 ft) in diameter and has double thick walls. It is reinforced by 16 radial nerves and encircled by ten iron chains that absorb pressure from above.

Baldachin Built by Bernini, it is located above the central altar which, at the same time, is the probable tomb of Saint Peter. Its four Solomon-styled columns are decorated with a Baroque emblem.

Inscription The words of Jesus are written in Latin in the frieze: 'You are Peter and upon this stone I will build my church.' A staircase of 537 steps passes around it and continues up to the summit.

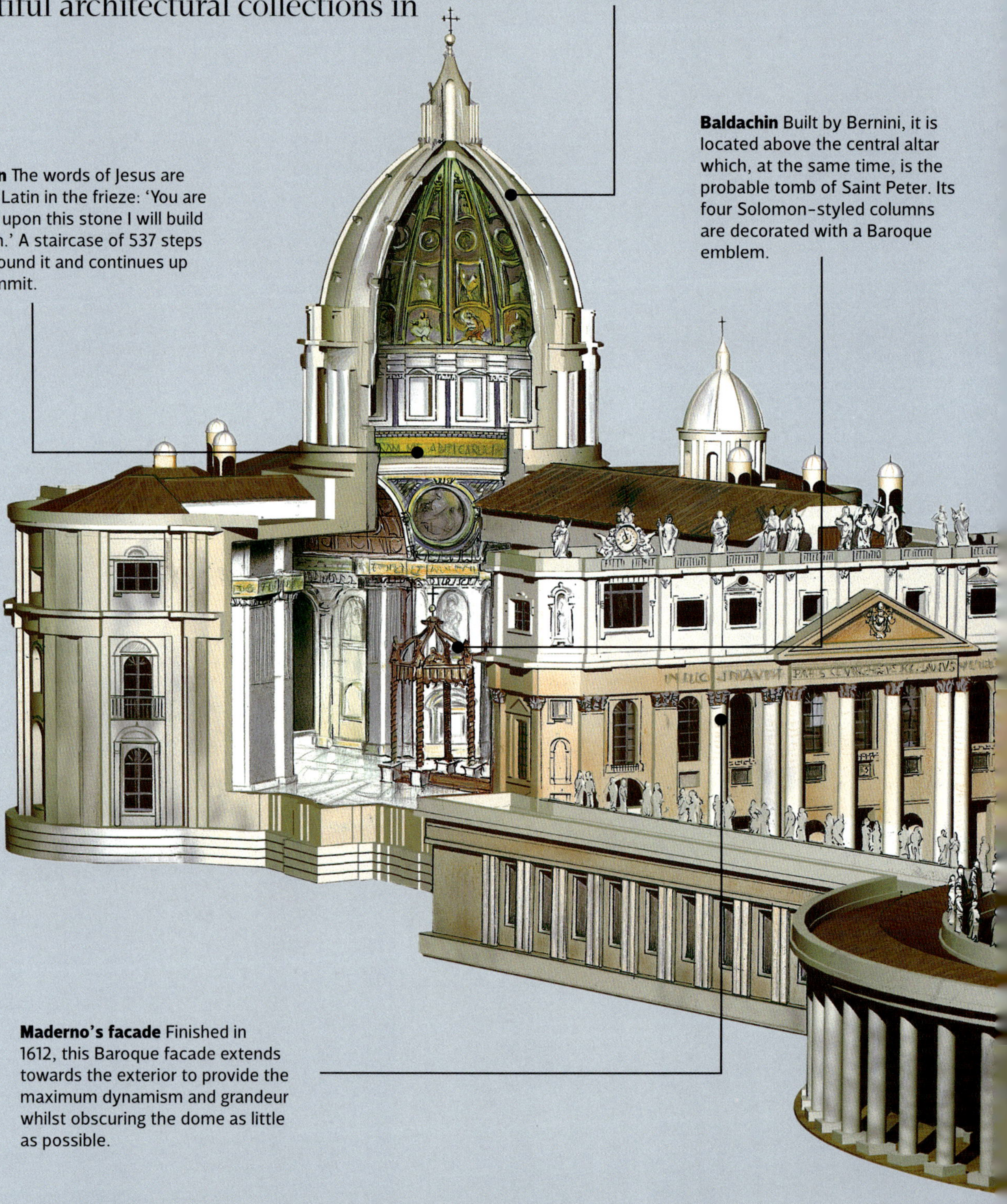

Maderno's facade Finished in 1612, this Baroque facade extends towards the exterior to provide the maximum dynamism and grandeur whilst obscuring the dome as little as possible.

The final structure In addition to the facade, Carlo Maderno participated in the conversion of the original Greek cross floor plan into a larger Roman cross floor plan. The square conceived by Bernini was designed to accommodate the larger number of faithful and to enhance the dome, somewhat hidden behind the new facade.

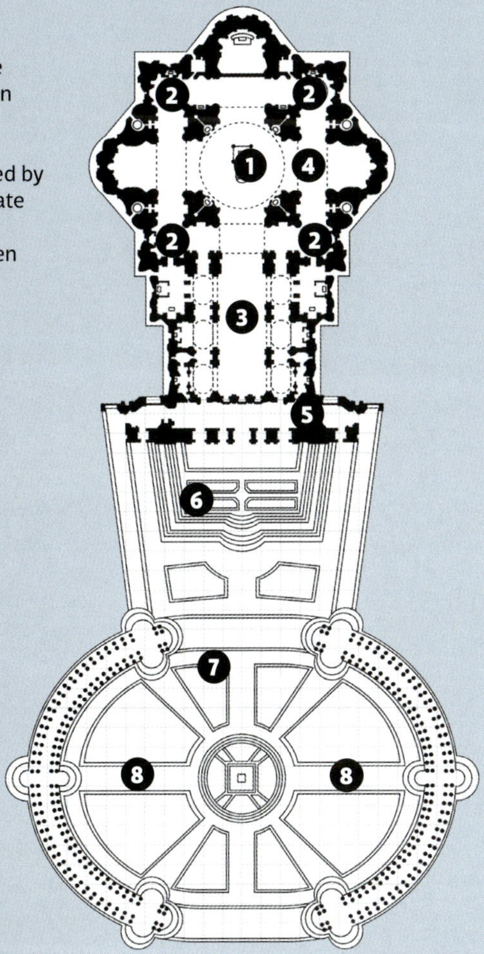

1. Altar and baldachin
2. Dome pillars
3. Main nave
4. Transverse nave
5. Maderno facade
6. Access staircase
7. Bernini square
8. Fountains

Egyptian obelisk Brought to Rome by Caligula in 36 BC it was transferred and erected here in 1586 by the Pope as a symbol of the triumph of Christianity over paganism.

Diverging walls These two facing walls are a continuation of those which are located in front of the colonnades creating an optical illusion which makes the facade and dome appear larger.

Holy sculptures Along the balustrade, above the columns which face the square, there are 140 sculptures which represent Christian saints.

The colonnade These 296 columns of the Doric order are narrower than usual and grouped in four lines, in effect creating an impenetrable forest from all viewpoints.

TAJ MAHAL

Agra This imposing mausoleum stands in the city of Agra, in the state of Uttar Pradesh, 200 km (124 mi) to the south of Delhi, close to the river Yamuna.

Monument to love

A paradigm of Moghul art and one of the most significant buildings in the history of architecture, the Taj Mahal is a large mausoleum erected in honour of the wife of the Emperor Shah Jahan.

In the history of art there is an infinity of paintings, sculptures, poems and songs inspired by the love their authors felt for their beloved, but none of them have the magnitude of the Taj Mahal, the monumental mausoleum that the Emperor Shah Jahan had built in the middle of the 17th century to house the body of Mumtaz Mahal, his favourite wife.

At the beginning of the 16th century, the Mongol heirs of the legendary Khan (Emperor) Tamburlaine, under pressure from other ethnic groups in Central Asia, were obliged to cross the magnificent mountain range of the Hindu Kush, and they conquered a large part of the Indian subcontinent, founding the so-called Moghul Empire, which dominated India until the beginning of the 18th century. Akbar, the second and most powerful of the Moghul Emperors, set up his court at Agra, on the banks of the river Yamuna, in the present-day state of Uttar Pradesh. His descendant Jahangir administered an empire that was stable and flourishing, which allowed him to dedicate himself to provide his court with intense cultural activity. Although he would end up in conflict with his son Shah Jahan (1592–1666), the fifth Moghul Emperor, he grew up in this opulent and refined atmosphere. It is not so strange, then, that when moved by an uncontrollable and ill-fated love, Shah Jahan should decide to build a mausoleum whose richness of construction and decoration has no equal in the world, either at that time or today. In fact, the excesses produced by the family's spiral of opulence and ostentation were one of the main reasons for the rapid decline of the empire of the Moghuls, which ended up as a small kingdom near Delhi in the early days of British rule.

The best architects in the service of an idea

The ascent of Shah Jahan to the throne was no bed of roses. To achieve power he had to cut himself off from his family and send his stepmother into exile. In this situation, the new Emperor placed all his affection on his wife, the Persian princess Arjumand Banu Begum, who he called Mumtaz Mahal, 'the chosen one of the palace' in Farsi. They were engaged in 1607, when he was 15

↑Details The friezes in the upper part of the arches are sculpted panels.

↗Combined styles The Taj Mahal includes elements from Islamic and Arab tradition, such as the minarets that stand at the four corners.

and she was 14, and married five years later. In their 19 years of marriage, Mumtaz had 14 children with Shah Jahan, and died in childbirth with the last of these, aged 38, leaving an enormous hole in the life of the Emperor.

Disconsolate, Shah Jahan soon commenced construction of a mausoleum in Agra whose beauty would do justice to the love he felt for his deceased wife, and he devoted unlimited resources to the project. During the life of Mumtaz Mahal, the Emperor had already ordered palaces and gardens for her, like those of Shalimar in Lahore (now in Pakistan); the tomb at Agra was to put everything built up until that point in the shade. For this work, Shah Jahan called on the most prestigious architects and craftsmen in the world, and committed himself personally to the project too, developing his own ideas. The specialist in designing bulbous domes came from Istanbul, while the finish was achieved by technical experts from Lahore and Samarkand. The delicate calligraphy was the work of artists from Baghdad and the landscapers and gardeners came from Bukhara and Kashmir. As many as 20,000 workers were involved in the construction, which lasted 17 years.

Inspired by the Timur and Moghul architectural traditions from Central Asia, and with significant Arab influences transmitted through the Persians, the Taj Mahal, the pinnacle of Moghul art, is a funerary monument situated next to the river and set in gardens whose cross-shaped pools add perspective to the complex and reflect the white marble that covers the whole building, changing tone according to the time of day you see it. On either side of the tomb there is a

↑Inlays The designs on the floor are made with semi-precious stones inlaid in the marble.

↗Mosque The interior of the mosque is decorated with floral motives, which symbolise paradise for Muslims.

→Dome The dome is six storeys high and has the onion shape typical of Islam, as later used in Russia.

↑Filigrees Filigree decorations are everywhere inside and outside the Taj Mahal.

mosque and an inn to welcome visitors, and with the entrance gates this completes a complex of buildings whose symmetry transmits serenity and perfection.

However, the key to the building is its refined decoration. As Islam prohibits figurative images, all the marble slabs are ornamented with an infinity of delicately inlaid abstract forms, made of semi-precious stones – like jade and lapis lazuli; amber, coral, rock crystals and black stone, with floral motifs – a symbol of divine power for the Muslims; geometrical elements and calligraphic inscriptions with verses from the Koran. Inside, the decoration reaches the zenith of opulence, thanks to the extensive use of precious and semi-precious stones. The symmetry of the whole has been slightly altered by the subsequent addition of the cenotaph of Shah Jahan himself, who shortly after the completion of the work, in 1658, fell ill and was removed from power by his sons, passing the rest of his days shut up in the fort of Agra. At his death, aged 74, he could finally lie next to his beloved for the rest of eternity.

Pinnacle of Moghul art

This great funerary monument is outstanding for its combination of shapes and spaces, its rich decoration and the symmetry of the complex.

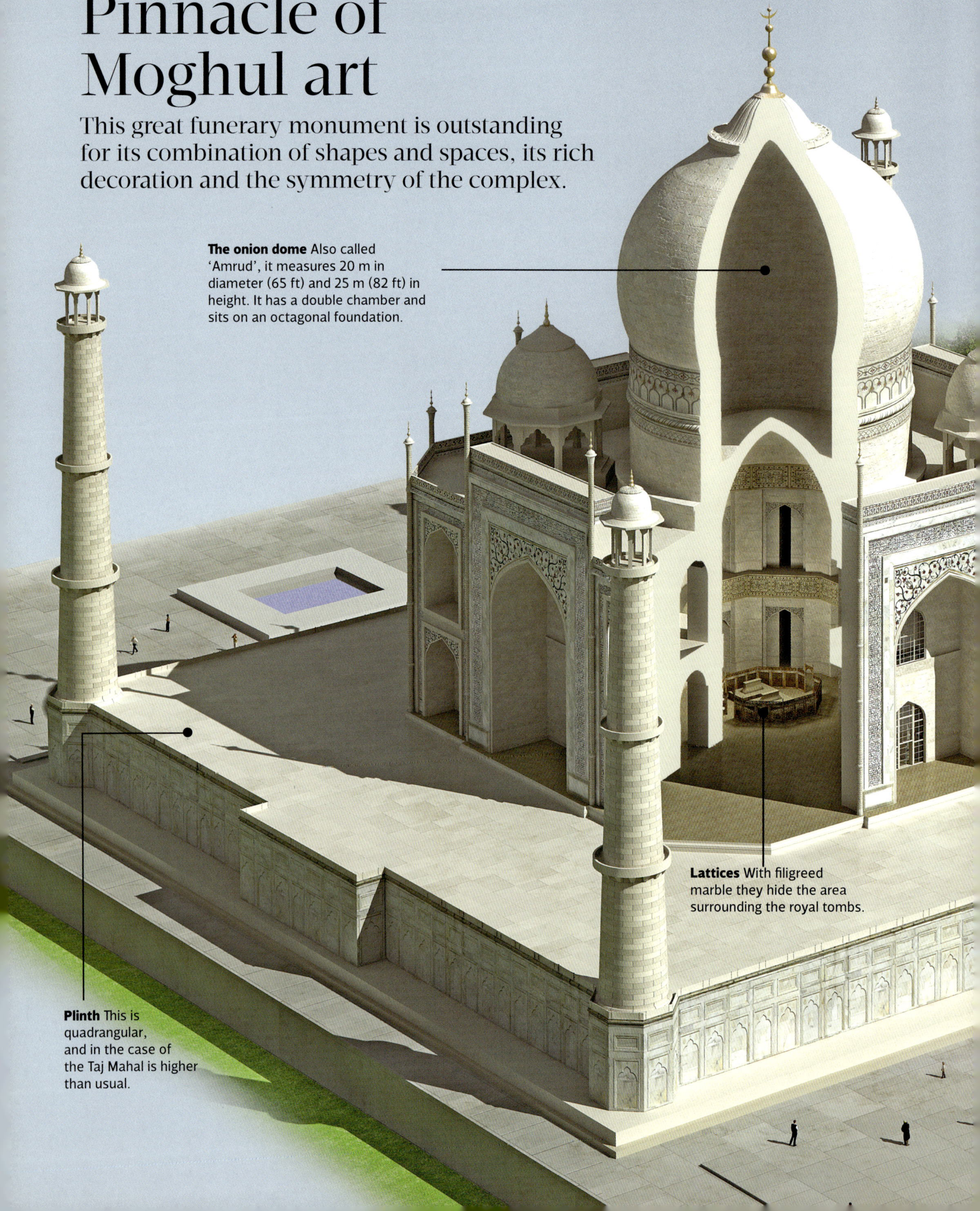

The gardens Measuring 567 m by 305 m (1,860 ft by 1,000 ft), they have more than one hundred types of plants and are divided into four parts by canals that cross in the middle, and in turn each of the resulting rectangles is subdivided into another four, to make a total of 16 areas.

Four minarets Each one is 40 m (131 ft) high and is crowned by an octagonal prayer balcony or *chatri*. They surround the tomb and highlight the perfect symmetry of the complex.

Symmetry Unlike other Moghul tombs, the Taj Mahal was placed at the end of the garden and not in the middle. In this way, it was ensured that nobody could ever build anything behind it and alter the image of the mausoleum.

EMPIRE STATE BUILDING

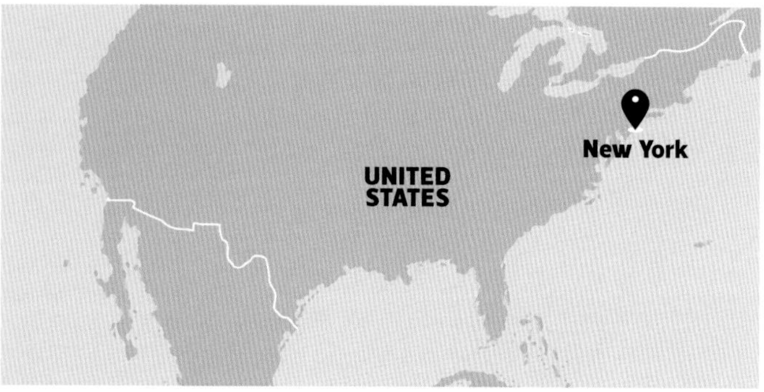

New York Located in the heart of Manhattan, the Empire State Building is one of the icons of the North American city of New York.

Defying vertigo

Standing 443 m (1,453 ft) high and with 102 floors, this building was, for more than 40 years between 1931 and 1972, the tallest in the world.

Covering an area similar to Jersey or Guernsey, in the Channel Islands, the island of Manhattan was the birthplace of New York. Dutch settlers arrived there at the beginning of the 17th century. This extraordinary location, and the magnificent conditions of its natural port, encouraged the population to grow progressively, from 80,000 inhabitants in 1800 to 3.5 million a century later. This accelerated demographic growth promoted the expansion of the city towards the areas outside the Hudson Estuary and a meteoric increase in the price of land in Manhattan. This led the municipal authorities to lift regulations which, for safety reasons, limited the height of structures, in order to take maximum advantage of the surface area available for the buildings designed at the beginning of the 19th century.

Born in Chicago, the revolution which signified the application of new materials such as steel, reinforced concrete and glass in immense built structures, as well as the invention of the lift by American engineer Elisha Otis, allowed 19th-century architects to design increasingly taller buildings. From the end of the 19th century and especially during the 1930s of the following century, there was a mad rush in New York to develop the tallest building: the World Building, which no longer exists, was built in 1890 and had 20 floors. This was superseded in 1899 by the now rather modest Park Row Building, built with 30 floors. The Metropolitan Life Tower, which was completed in 1909, reached a respectable 50 floors and a height of 213 m (69 ft) but was superseded just four years later by the Woolworth building, a spectacular 241 m (791 ft) tower built in a neo-Gothic style.

An art deco giant

Curiously, the Crash of 1929, the period of decline known as the Great Depression which extended to the end of World War II, didn't just have no affect on this race to reach the New York sky, but accelerated it. In 1930, the marvellous Chrysler building, culminating in a resplendent stainless steel spire inspired by the hubcaps of the Chrysler car was built. However, the reign of the

↑Al fresco cleaning Initially, the skyscraper's windows were cleaned one by one, by specialists attached to the frames by a harness.

Chrysler building, a paragon of art deco style, lasted just 11 months. On 1 May 1931, on the corner of Fifth Avenue and West 34th Street, another art deco giant was unveiled: the Empire State Building. This new king of New York, and indeed the planet, measures 443 m (1,453 ft) – 381 m (1,250 ft) to the roof – and has 102 floors reached by 73 lifts. Named after the nickname of New York State, the Empire State building was, for more than 40 years, between 1931 and 1972, the tallest in the world, and for more than a decade – between 2001 and 2012 – it reclaimed first place amongst the New York skyscrapers after the terrible destruction of the two World Trade Centre towers in the terrorist attacks of September 11. Located on a midtown Manhattan site, which was previously the site of the Waldorf Astoria Hotel, and covering a wide base which gets narrower as it gets taller, the Empire State Building was designed by the American architect William Frederick Lamb (1883–1952), designer of other unique New York buildings such as the headquarters of the oil company Standard Oil, the Bankers Trust, the magazine Forbes and the famous building at 521 Fifth Avenue. For the design of the new office skyscrapers, Lamb took two recently finished buildings as inspiration: Carew Tower of Cincinnati and the Reynolds building, of Winston-Salem.

This style was very popular among the elite bourgeoisie of the west between the two World Wars and was inspired by the rationalism of the German Bauhaus school and the first avant-garde movements, especially Cubism, Futurism and Constructivism . It is characterised by the use of blunt lines and solid symmetrical and geometric forms, using new materials such as steel, aluminium and lacquers. The Empire State's wonderful lobby, covering three floors, is where the art deco

↑Icon Owing to its architecture and having appeared in many films, the building is synonymous with the 'Big Apple'.

↗Renovation In 2009, 500 million dollars were invested in renovating the lobby and the communal areas in order to return them to their former splendour.

→The Large Base Occupies an area greater than 8,000 m^2 (26,247 ft^2).

↑Observation deck Owing to several suicides, it was decided to incorporate a protective mesh over the observation deck of the 86th floor.

decor is most evident, although the influences of this style cover common elements on all floors, including the finish of the building which was worthy of the film *Metropolis*, an icon of expressionism and futurism which was released three years before work commenced.

To build this colossus it was necessary to hire 3,500 workers, the majority of whom were European immigrants who worked for 410 days, at a rate of 4.5 floors per week, although during the maximum period of productivity 14 floors were built in just 10 days. Hundreds of blacksmiths from the Mohawk tribe, experts in steel and iron works came down, from the Canadian indigenous reserve of Kahnawake, and also worked on the construction. Since its opening, between 20,000 and 25,000 employees work in the building every day which, after the Pentagon, is the second largest office complex in the United States. However, it was perhaps the giant gorilla King Kong who made it the most famous skyscraper in the world by scaling the outside of the building in the final scene of the 1933 film.

MACYS

Reaching the sky

More than 80 years after its opening, the most famous skyscraper in the world continues to act as an essential reference point for international architecture.

THE TALLEST BUILDINGS

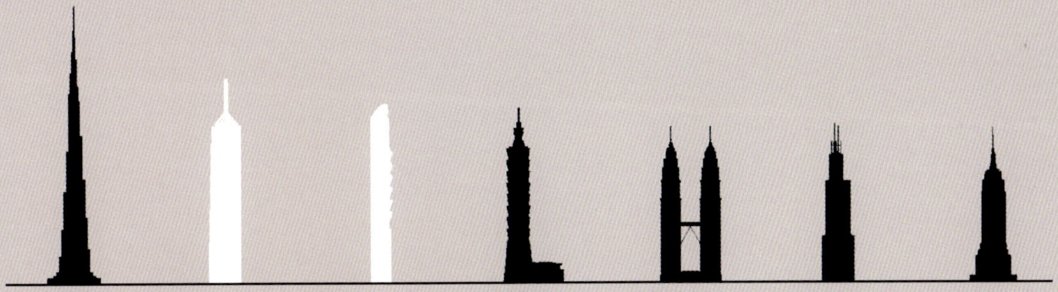

818 m (2,684 ft) Burj Dubai, Dubai

541 m (2,684 ft) One World Trade Center, USA

516 m (1,693 ft) Pentominium, Dubai

508 m (1,667 ft) Taipei 101, Taiwan

452 m (1,483 ft) Petronas Towers, Malaysia

442 m (1,450 ft) Sears Tower, USA

381 m (1,250 ft) Empire State Building, USA

UNDER CONSTRUCTION

Observation deck On the 86th floor there is an open-air observation deck protected by glass.

Lights Since 1964, the upper floors of the building have had coloured lights which shine during holidays such as Christmas and Thanksgiving, sporting victories and other events.

Dizzyingly large numbers The building has 70 lifts, 113 km (70 miles) of tubes, 760,000 m (2,493,438 ft) of electric cable and around 9,000 taps.

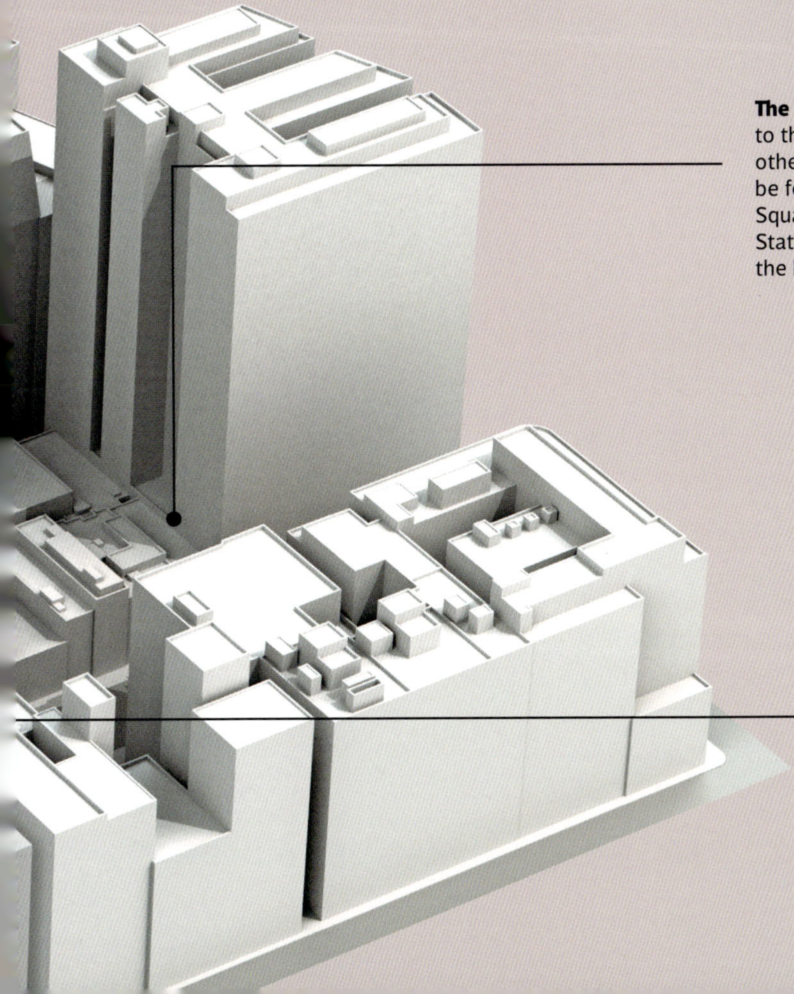

The surrounding area Close to the Empire State Building other icons of the city can be found, such as Madison Square Garden, Penn Station, Herald Square and the New York Public Library.

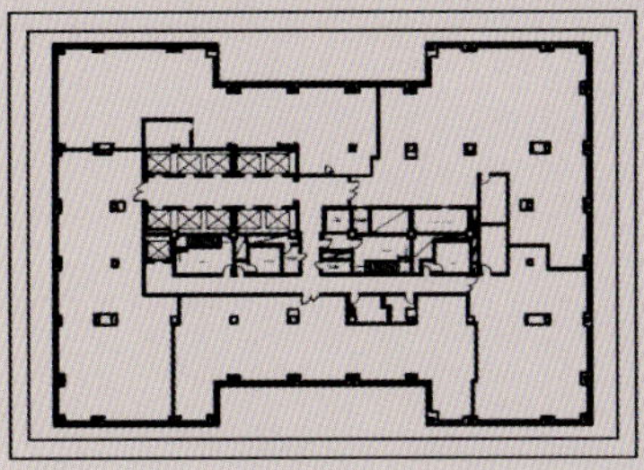

Offices The building has 200,500 m^2 (2,158,155 ft^2) of office and commercial space. It houses almost 1,000 companies and has its own postcode.

SYDNEY OPERA HOUSE

Sydney On the shores of Sydney Bay, the financial capital of Australia, stands a masterpiece of contemporary architecture.

The city's icon

Despite the difficulties involved in the construction of the unique and spectacular vaults that cover the complex, the Sydney Opera House is one of the most emblematic buildings of the 20th century.

What does it cost to have an emblematic building in the city? How much do you have to pay a great architect to have him put all his creativity into the design of that project? Are the financial benefits of an iconic building worthwhile for a city? These questions were asked by Sydney for a long time before it was decided, in 1957, to commission the construction of a large opera auditorium by Danish designer Jørn Utzon. Certainly the road was difficult, and the city's reserves were exhausted after construction, but today no inhabitant of the capital of New South Wales can say that the decision to build the marvellous Sydney Opera House was a bad one.

Utzon's creation is an indisputable icon of 20th-century world architecture that far exceeded the expectations of the city's authorities when the project was conceived. Since its unveiling, the Sydney Opera House has become the symbol of the city. It is sufficient to type 'Sydney' into an image search engine to understand the weight the building carries in terms of the city's marketing. The Opera House is to Sydney what the Eiffel Tower is to Paris. What are the financial implications of the constant appearance of Utzon's work on the social networks and digital and editorial publications of the world? They have certainly far exceeded what was initially predicted, as did the final cost and duration of the work, that for decades tainted the architectural values of the building. Work began in 1959, with completion expected in 1965, but the Opera House wasn't opened until 1973. Over these 14 years of construction, the initial budget was exceeded by 1,400 per cent!

A path strewn with obstacles

The eventful history of this unique building began in 1949 when an intense debate opened concerning the need for a large and flourishing country, such as Australia, to have an opera theatre which could compete with the classic settings of the West. Society's enthusiasm for the idea was such that the eventual economic limits of the project were secondary. In 1955, a meeting was held which discussed the construction of a

↑Sails The domes of the Sydney Opera House open out on to the sea from Bennelong Point, as if they form the rigging of a sailing ship.

large opera theatre on the peninsula of Bennelong Point, a privileged position at the entrance of the magnificent Sydney Bay.

Despite the regulations requiring candidates to provide detailed structural plans and calculations that would allow construction to begin immediately, Danish architect Jørn Utzon, an outstanding student of Finn Alvar Aalto and admirer of American Frank Lloyd Wright, submitted a simple drawing on which the vaults in the form of sails, an allegory of the marine and naval environment of the extraordinary location, could be clearly seen. However, the almost magical effect of this unique design allowed him to defeat all opposition and win the competition due to his special vision of integrating architecture into the environment. Construction began in 1959. Problems began to arise soon after the demolition of the Sydney Tram Depot – which had been built to emulate the old Fort Macquarie which occupied the site until 1901 – and the construction of the podium on which the building would sit. The pillars which had to support the cover were constructed without knowing its weight. And the vaults – so eye – catching on paper – became a nightmare for the engineers, led by the famous Ove Arup. Utzon had thought that the formwork would be carried out in situ, but this solution would have been even slower and more expensive. Finally, prefabricated concrete panels were made which were connected by pre–stressed steel rods and covered in ceramic tiles that reflect sunlight. The extreme difficulty in constructing the curves of the enormous vaults required the use of computers for the first time in the history of architecture.

Resignation of Utzon

The problems of the vaults overcome, and with construction already behind schedule, the change

↑Interior Inside view of the Sydney Opera House complex with the windows that open out onto the bay.

→Incomparable From the sea, the unmistakable Opera Theatre stands out proudly against the backdrop of the rest of the city's buildings.

↑Vaults More than one million white and beige tiles cover the building's vaults.

↗Access Image of the staircase that gives access to the cultural complex.

of government in New South Wales state brought a reduction in the budget of the Opera House and the immediate resignation of Utzon. The architect completely washed his hands of the project prior to the construction of the inside which comprised a concert hall for 2,700 spectators, an Opera Theatre for 1,500 people and a theatre for dramatic works with 550 seats, in addition to other rooms.

In 1973, Sydney was finally able to enjoy a surprising expressionist building which would forge the way for complex geometric forms in construction, a route later explored by architects such as Frank Gehry in buildings such as the Guggenheim Museum Bilbao. At the end of the 1990s, the Opera House board encouraged a reconciliation with Utzon with the aim of remodelling the building. The investiture of the Danish architect as an honorary doctor by the University of Sydney in 2003, five years before his death, restored the harmony between the designer of a key 20th-century building and the city which welcomed it.

AMP
AMP
AMP

An architectural milestone

With eight stages – one of which is open air – the Sydney Opera House is one of the most visited structures in the city: seven million people pass through its doors each year.

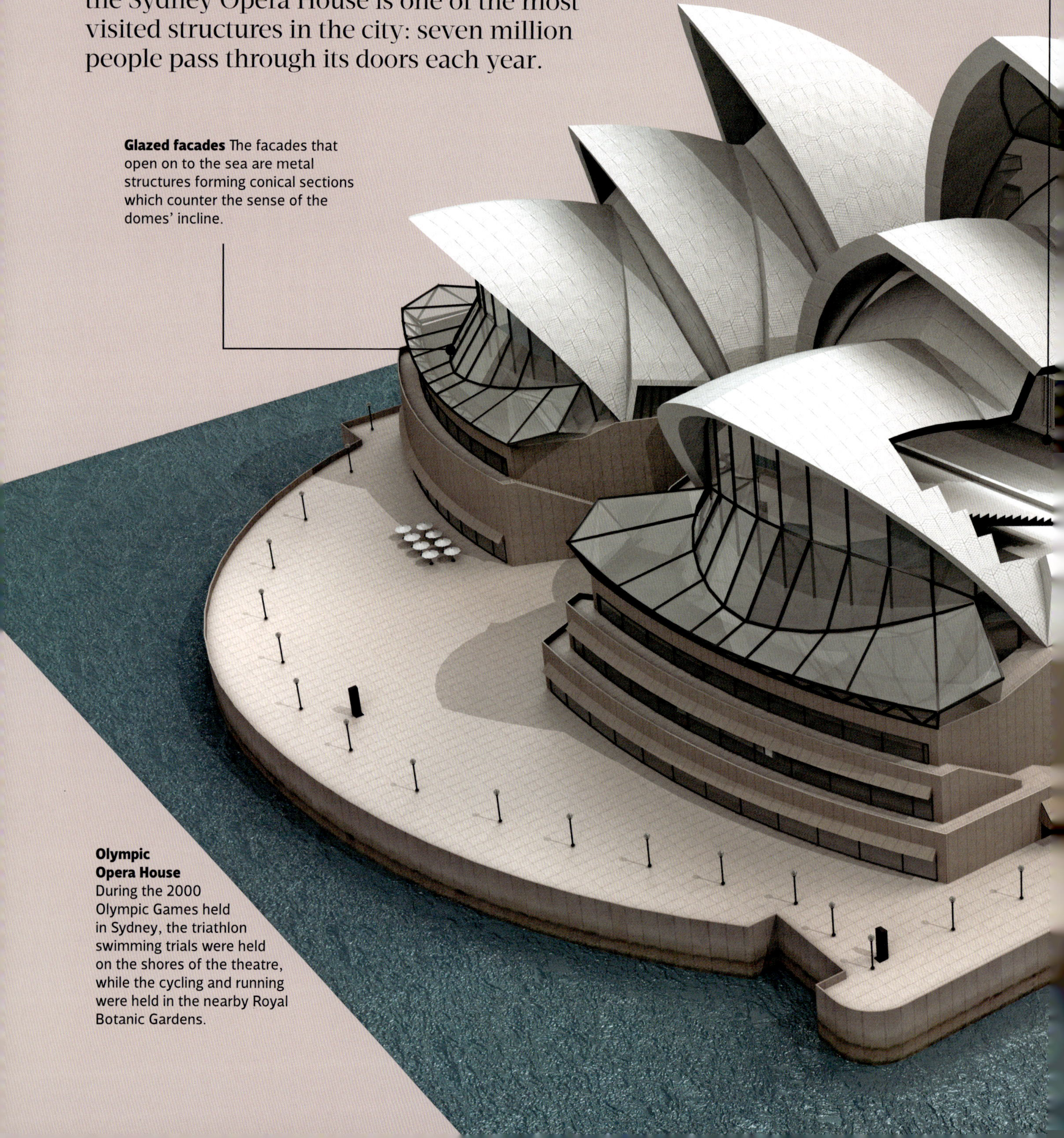

The cupolas They were built wtih prefabricated concrete panels supported with concrete ribs. The cover is made up of white and cream-coloured ceramic tiles.

Joan Sutherland Theatre Named in honour of the Australian soprano, this 1,500-seater space was originally designed for the symphony, but changes in the design converted it into the opera, theatre and ballet hall.

Australian diva Joan Sutherland (1926–2010) was one of the most important sopranos of the 20th century.

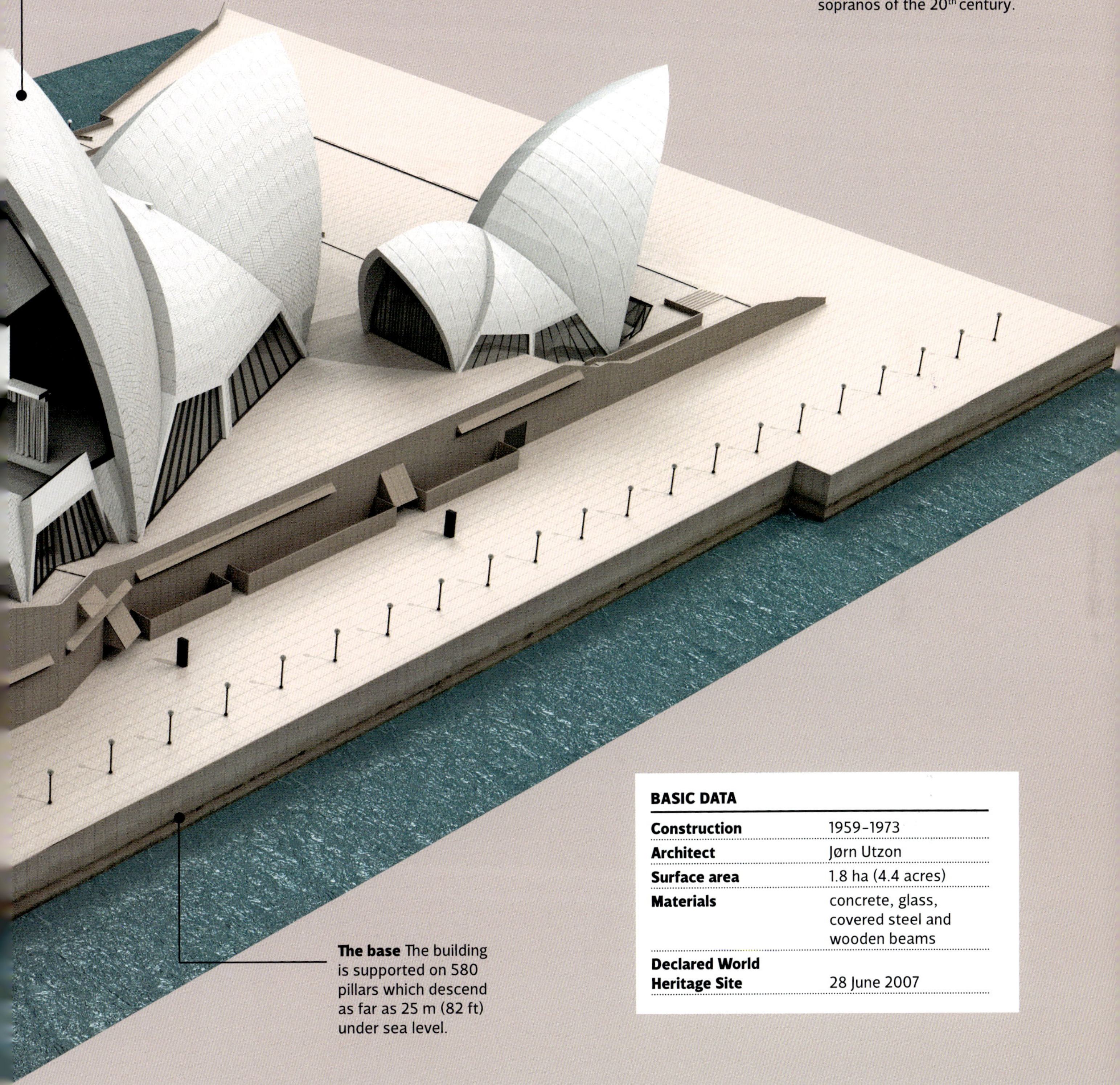

The base The building is supported on 580 pillars which descend as far as 25 m (82 ft) under sea level.

BASIC DATA	
Construction	1959–1973
Architect	Jørn Utzon
Surface area	1.8 ha (4.4 acres)
Materials	concrete, glass, covered steel and wooden beams
Declared World Heritage Site	28 June 2007

WONDERS OF NATURE

Paradise in its pure state

Nature puts on the greatest show on earth: the movement of tectonic plates and atmospheric phenomena have modified and moulded the Earth's surface to configure a great variety of unique landscapes and ecosystems. From the snowy peaks of the Himalayas or Kilimanjaro to the sculpted rocks of the Grand Canyon, from the great waterfalls of Iguazu to the volcanic islands of the Galapagos, from the harsh desert climate of the Sahara to the humid, tropical jungle of Amazonia, there are still some real paradises on our planet, where nature can express herself with all her intensity, and where life emerges in its most varied forms... Discover this beautiful planet.

ANTARCTICA

Antarctica Home to the South Pole, this continent is governed by the Antarctic Treaty, which has 50 signatory countries, although only 28 have the right to vote.

White giant

Cold, dry, deserted and windy, the Antarctic, free from national sovereignty and seriously threatened by climate change, is the last virgin land on the planet.

Continental drift has meant that our era coincides with an enormous land mass passing over the South Pole. This situation, which began just 50 million years ago – the Earth is 4,600 million years old – has transformed this continent – the Antarctic – into the most unique and extreme place on earth. It is the coldest, driest, windiest, most isolated and virgin land in the world, characteristics which make it a fascinating place, the last frontier for humanity within our own world.

Located some 1000 km (600 mi) off South America, the Antarctic is, without doubt, the most remote land on the planet. All other continents are located less than 100 km (54 mi) from another land mass. This isolation explains why, despite its enormous size – much larger than Europe and Oceania – the Antarctic wasn't discovered until 1773 when the ship, HMS *Resolution*, captained by the British explorer James Cook, became the first boat to cross the Antarctic Circle and hit the ice floes.

The first landing on the Antarctic mainland didn't happen until 1824, and it wasn't until the beginning of the 20th century that the frozen continent became the main objective for exploration attempts, some of which became ordeals. In 1911, two expeditions, one Norwegian, led by Roald Amundsen, and one British, under Robert Scott, left a few days apart with the same goal: to reach the geographical South Pole located at the centre of the continent. Eventually Amundsen, equipped with sledges pulled by dogs from Greenland, arrived at the pole on the 14 December, one month before Scott, who died on the return journey along with the rest of his expedition.

Scientific interest

Today, more than one hundred years after those heroic deeds, just 1,000 people live in the Antarctic all year round, all incorporated into the 100 scientific stations from 26 countries which operate on the continent, working on investigations relating to climate and meteorology and the study of the particular geology

↑**Animal-drawn transport** Until the appearance of vehicles in the 20th century, a sledge, pulled by dogs from Greenland, was the only method of transport used on the continent.

and biology of this land of records: the average temperature is -17°C, and the coldest and lowest ever recorded on the planet was taken on 21 July 1980 at the Russian Vostock base, which reached -89.3°C! The sensation of extreme cold is accentuated by the winds that lash the region almost constantly. In 1972, the wind gauge at the French research station Dumont d'Urville recorded gusts of up to 327 km/h (203 mph). The cold and wind are two factors that make Antarctica the driest continent in the world. Contrary to what most might expect, the atmospheric dryness can exceed that recorded in the most arid deserts on the planet. There are regions, such as the McMurdo Dry Valleys, in which the environment is so extremely dry that the surface lacks the characteristic covering of ice, the average thickness of which is 2.4 km (1.5 mi) over the entire continent, with a maximum of almost 5 km (3 mi), which is primarily submerged below sea level. The extreme conditions in the Dry Valleys allow many scientists who work in this region to emulate the environment on Mars and investigate the possibilities of the red planet hosting life.

Wildlife on ice

The reality is that life finds a way, even in such adverse circumstances. The Antarctic has limited wildlife concentrated on the coasts, examples of which include: the Emperor Penguin, the largest in its family, with its clumsy gait, is capable of walking between 50 and 100 km (31 and 62 mi) over the ice to the interior in order to mate and incubate its eggs; the Antarctic Cod, whose blood has an anti-freeze protein; the Leopard seal; the Weddell seal; the blue whale; the giant squid, and numerous birds such as the Antarctic skua, the giant petrel and the Antarctic cormorant. There are forms of life so adapted to the prevailing harsh

↑Port Lockroy The former British research station on Wiencke Island today houses one of four Antarctic museums.

↗Climate change Antarctica is the region most affected by the hole in the ozone layer.

→On the coast The Adelie penguin *(Pygoscelis adeliae)* and the Emperor Penguin are the only two penguins that live on the mainland.

↑Danger Burgeoning tourism is beginning to alter the fragile equilibrium of the Antarctic ecosystem.

conditions that they are capable of living in the dark under 190 m (623 ft) of ice, such as a small crustacean from the Lysianassidae family, and a type of jellyfish. In addition to this interesting wildlife, the Antarctic has vast mineral resources – oil, uranium, iron, carbon, gold, chromium – which are not exploited in accordance with the Antarctic Treaty signed in 1959 by the 12 countries which claim to have territorial rights to the continent. This Treaty puts Antarctica outside any national sovereignty, prohibits military activities and economic exploitation and preserves the region for scientific research.

Despite this agreement, the continent is not free from the dangers of human activity. As a result of climate change, global warming is accelerating the melting of the ice barriers that occupy the enormous bays of the Antarctic coast. It must be noted that the continent contains 80 per cent of the planet's fresh water. If the ice melts it will cause an increase of up to 60 m (197 ft) in sea level.

Antarctic wildlife

Although many animals live temporarily on the coasts of the Antarctic, where they feed and breed, only the penguins and some species of fish are permanent residents.

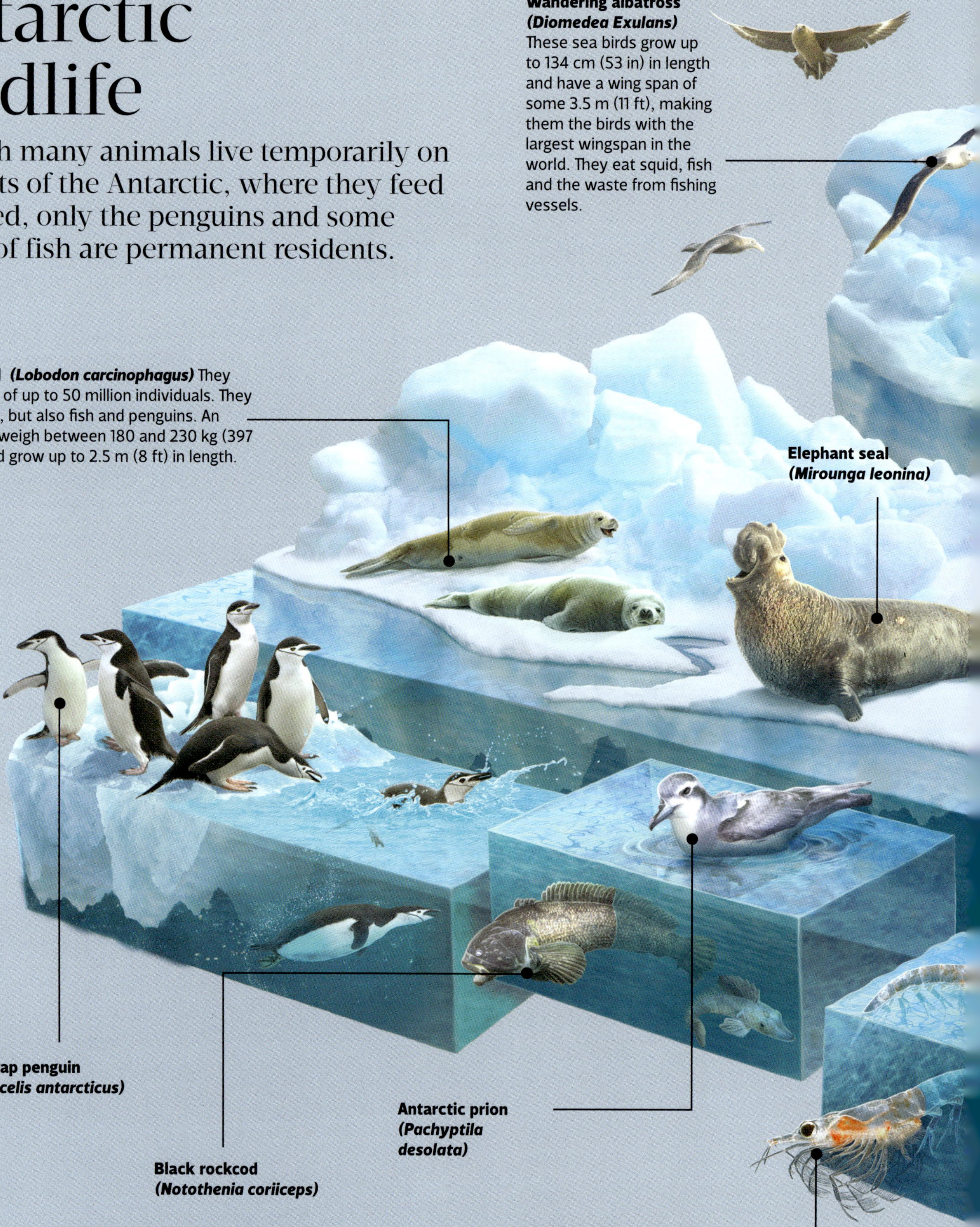

Killer whale *(Orcinus orca)* Killer whales hunt warm-blooded animals in packs. They locate their prey on the ice floes and, with their sharp teeth, tear at the flesh.
Sperm whale *(Physeter macrocephalus)* Sperm whales are the largest living carnivores on the planet. They can be found throughout the world except the Arctic and usually go on long migratory journeys. The males travel to the Antarctic to find food.
Antarctic minke whale *(Balaenoptera bonaerensis)* The minke whale is the smallest of the cetaceans. It feeds using its baleen, bristles which filter the water and retain food, mainly krill.
Leopard seal *(Hydrurga leptonyx)*
Gentoo penguin *(Pygoscelis papua)*
Emperor penguin *(Aptenodytes forsteri)* These penguins can grow up to one metre (3.3 ft) in height and weigh 45 kg (99 lb). They are the largest species of penguin in the world.

THE GALAPAGOS ISLANDS

Galapagos Islands This archipelago situated on the Pacific Ocean some 1,000 km (621 mi) from the coast of South America, administratively belongs to Ecuador.

Darwin's dream

A habitat for a multitude of unique endemic species, the Galapagos Islands form an open-air laboratory which helped Darwin to develop the Theory of Evolution.

On the 27 December 1831, a British naturalist called Charles Darwin set off on a five-year round-the-world scientific expedition at the age of 22 on the Royal Navy bring HMS *Beagle*, captained by Robert Fitzroy. The ship crossed the Atlantic, circumnavigated South America and set a course for Oceania via the Pacific.

One of the *Beagle's* ports of call through the largest of the oceans on the planet was the Galapagos Islands, an uninhabited archipelago of volcanic origin situated 1,000 km (386 mi) to the west of Ecuador. It was discovered in the 16th century by a Spanish bishop and since 1832 – three years before the arrival of Darwin – was administered by the then recently emancipated Ecuadorian government. The revolutionary English biologist, who had already made some surprising scientific discoveries on the American continent, found the Galapagos Islands an ideal setting for his investigations on the evolution of species, which would radically overturn the ideas held until then concerning the origin of man.

Formed in the wake of several underwater eruptions at a hot spot where three tectonic plates converge, the Galapagos archipelago was, and continues to be, a volcanic land continually renewed, with barely any vegetation, and on which wildlife arriving by air or by sea on long migrations from far-away lands established itself.

An open-air laboratory

Isolated from the rest of the world, these animals evolved to the rhythm of this unique substratum, adapting themselves to living conditions different to those their ancestors had in their places of origin. With the passage of time, these communities became new species, very different to those that had colonised the islands tens or hundreds of thousands of years earlier. Thus, on his arrival in the Galapagos Islands, Darwin found a world that was completely unheard of in Europe, complete with strange animals removed from the conventions he had learned about in England.

↑Bartholomew Island One of the smallest of the archipelago, just 1.2 km^2 (0.5 mi^2); it is possible to go scuba diving and penguin watching here.

↗Sally Lightfoot crabs These live on lava rocks and eat algae and small animals. To do this they follow the cycle of the tide.

During the month Darwin was on the islands – from September to October 1835 – the British naturalist collected examples of local wildlife, drew and described the different species he found with precision and noted the differences between the individuals of the archipelago and those of the continent, and even between those of the different islands. He saw, for example, that the giant tortoise that inhabited the region had a different shell according to the vegetation on which it fed. On islands on which bushes of a certain height predominated, the shell had an arch which allowed the tortoise to extend its neck to reach the branches. However, on the islands on which low bushes predominated, this feature did not exist. On returning to England one year later, in 1836 – after visiting Tahiti and Australia – the naturalist also noticed the different shapes of the finches' beaks on the archipelago and concluded that these variations were also due to its diet, which in turn had adapted to the food available on each island.

The Theory of Evolution

These investigations formed the basis for the publication of his essay, 23 years after his return to Europe, *On the Origin of Species*, which became a tremendously popular book in which Darwin reasoned that the animals and plants present at that time were the result of a multitude of successive changes undergone by previous forms since the origin of life on Earth. His Theory of Evolution of Species by means of natural selection, one of the most

↖Giant tortoise Galapagos tortoises can grow up to 2 m (6 ft) and weigh more than 400 kg (882 lb).

↑Endemic species The Galapagos penguin is endemic to the islands and the only one which inhabits the northern hemisphere of the planet.

←Unique features Darwin proved that the land and marine iguanas on the Galapagos Islands evolved differently on different islands.

↑Volcanic cacti These only grow on the lava lands of Bartholomew island.

influential theories in the history of modern science, was developed in this open-air laboratory on the Galapagos Islands.

Natural paradise

Today, the Galapagos is a protected national park which includes its total land surface as well as the region of sea which surrounds the archipelago, adding up to a total surface area of 7,880 km² (3,043 mi²). This area, similar in size to the Hebrides in Scotland, is home to 25,000 people, which means a population density of just three inhabitants per square kilometre (0.4 mi²).

There are five large islands: Isabela, which covers 60% of the total surface area, Santa Cruz, Fernandina, Santiago and San Cristobal, as well as eight smaller islands and hundreds of islets and outcrops. Each island is the result of the formation of a single isolated volcanic cone, all except Isabela, the largest, which houses six volcanoes. Five of these are active, the tallest of which is Wolf standing 1,707 m (5,600 ft) high.

Surrounded by countryside replete with submerged craters, lava fields, black and white sandy beaches, scarce vegetation dominated mainly by mango swamps on the shores, cacti on the coast and ferns and chrysanthemums on the slopes, the wildlife is the real owner of the Galapagos Islands. Accustomed to living without predators, especially humans, the indigenous animals are not known for their speed: the Galapagos tortoise – famous for its large size and longevity; the land and marine iguanas – which take visitors back to remote worlds dominated by reptiles; the Galapagos sea lion and the Galapagos penguin, the only one of its kind that inhabits the equatorial region.

The enormous variety of birds is another aspect of the great natural heritage of this archipelago, a true paradise for ornithologists, who can observe up to 13 endemic species of finch, the lava gull, the Galapagos hawk, the brown-grey petrel – known locally as the *patapegada* – or the dwarf heron, also called the grey heron owing to the colour of its plumage.

Refuge for unique species

The biodiversity of the archipelago includes numerous endemic animal and plant species.

Land iguana
(Conolophus subcristatus)
Lava fields The islands' volcanoes regularly erupt. The lava fields create fascinating forms and textures.
Lava heron
(Butorides sundevalli)
Galapagos fur seal
(Arctocephalus galapagoensis)
Flightless cormorant
(Phalacrocorax harrisi)
Galapagos penguin
(Spheniscus mendiculus)
Green sea turtle
(Chelonia mydas)
Whale shark
(Rhincodon typus)

THE AMAZON

The Amazon The great Amazon rainforest spans nine South American countries, although the largest part of the forest, 60 per cent, is found in Brazil.

A paradise of biodiversity

The basin of the longest and mightiest river in the world is home to an extensive tropical rainforest, and is populated by a range of flora and fauna not found anywhere else on Earth.

Despite the fact that human activity has reduced the surface area at an accelerated rate over the last few decades, the Amazon rainforest is still the largest tropical rainforest in the world. Its survival – today severely threatened – is fundamental for the equilibrium of the biosphere and the future of humanity, as it is the largest concentration of biodiversity on the planet and an enormous absorber of carbon dioxide, the gas that causes the greenhouse effect and climate change.

It extends over more than 6 million km^2 (2.3 million mi^2), which would make the Amazon the seventh largest country in the world. Located in South America, between the Andes mountain range and the Atlantic Ocean, it occupies almost the entire basin of the Amazon, the largest and mightiest river on the planet. It has an extensive area of lowlands and plains covering the northern half of Brazil, the south of Colombia, the east of Ecuador and Peru, and the north of Bolivia.

Globally, the Amazon rainforest can be seen as a homogeneous ecosystem with defined features: an almost constant high temperature – around 27°C – and constant and torrential rain over the region caused by the trade winds blowing humidity from the Atlantic. This climate system generates a vast amount of vegetation and ecologists believe the Amazon is an ecosystem at its peak: this means it is in a period of maturity in which all geological resources – minerals in the ground – and biological resources – flora and fauna – are operating at maximum yield.

The energy cycle

All the oxygen that these millions of square miles of plants generate through photosynthesis is consumed through the respiration and other vital processes of the living creatures that inhabit the ecosystem. This closed energy cycle therefore belies the old truism that the Amazon rainforest is the 'green lung' of the planet, capable of renewing the oxygen of much of the Earth's atmosphere, and it isn't even the

↑On the banks of the river A várzea forest grows in the basin of the Amazon, the mightiest river in the world.

most extensive wooded area on Earth: the North American and Siberian Taiga cover a considerably larger area.

However, it is certain that the Amazon has the largest reserve of biological diversity on the planet. The region represents 40 per cent of the tropical rainforest in the world and is home to half of all known animal and vegetable species. This is in contrast to the above mentioned boreal Taiga, in which just one woodland species – usually a conifer – monopolises enormous areas of land. In just one hectare of Amazon rainforest, 300 different species of tree can be identified, and up to 650 species of beetle can be found on each one. In fact, the height and the leafiness of these trees allow life to be distributed over various levels, from the ground, where very little light reaches, to the canopy in the treetops, where the intense sunlight provokes the concentration of a great variety of fauna which never descend to lower levels.

Diversity and abundance

With such biodiversity, it's hardly surprising that the Amazon is considered the main source of pharmaceutical products. Around 80 per cent of medication used in western medicine has been synthesised based on products extracted from plants, fungi and animals from the Amazon basin. Despite the geographical, climatic and biological homogeneity displayed to an external observer, the Amazon rainforest is, in reality, a mosaic of very different kinds of tropical forest, distinguished according to the composition of the ground in which it is rooted, the coverage of vegetation, and rainfall which can be between 2,000 mm (79 in) per year in the driest regions and 8,000 mm (315 in) in the wettest. Greater humidity equals a greater diversity of flora and fauna. This variety within uniformity materialises in

↑The kapok tree This tree can grow up to 70 m (230 ft) in height.

↗Victoria regia The leaf of this aquatic plant can grow up to 2.5 m (8 ft) in diameter.

↗Insects It is thought that 80 per cent of Amazonian species are yet to be discovered.

→Canopy walkways These wooden walkways give you a bird's-eye view of the forest.

↑Frogs In the Brazilian Amazon alone, 600 species of frog have been catalogued.

an extensive network of national parks and protected areas, each with its own personality: Manu National Park, located at the foot of the Andes, in the Peruvian Amazon, the Amacayacu National Park, located in southern Colombia, the Jaú National Park in Brazil, the largest reserve of virgin rainforest in the world, and the Amazonian National Park, which covers the final stretch of the Tapajós River, the main southern tributary of the Amazon River, also in Brazil.

While natural processes foster a diversity of life forms and a complexity of ecosystems to ensure stability, human activity, on the other hand, tends to decrease biodiversity in order to favour single species, as seen in monocrop farming, which simplifies ecosystems and makes them more fragile. The overexploitation of tropical forests is accompanied by the burning of huge tracts of forest for the cultivation of soya which serves as a foodstuff for cattle. In addition, these predatory actions threaten the survival of the surrounding 330,000 indigenous people from 220 ethnic groups who live in the region.

Forest inhabitants

The Amazonian rainforest is characterised by the density of its vegetation and the height of some of its trees, which form four distinct levels each with its own ecosystem.

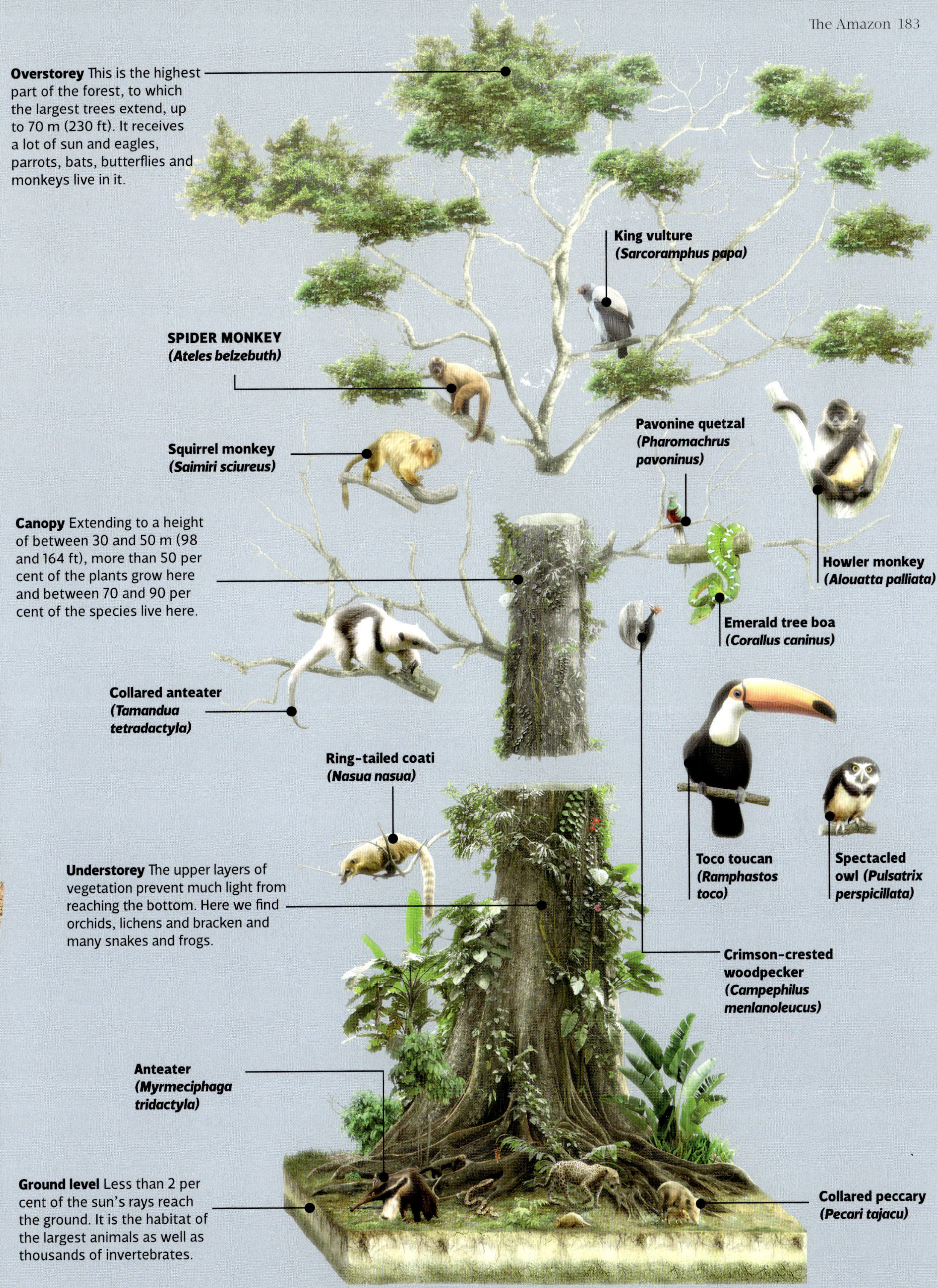
Overstorey This is the highest part of the forest, to which the largest trees extend, up to 70 m (230 ft). It receives a lot of sun and eagles, parrots, bats, butterflies and monkeys live in it.
King vulture ***(Sarcoramphus papa)***
SPIDER MONKEY ***(Ateles belzebuth)***
Squirrel monkey ***(Saimiri sciureus)***
Pavonine quetzal ***(Pharomachrus pavoninus)***
Canopy Extending to a height of between 30 and 50 m (98 and 164 ft), more than 50 per cent of the plants grow here and between 70 and 90 per cent of the species live here.
Howler monkey ***(Alouatta palliata)***
Emerald tree boa ***(Corallus caninus)***
Collared anteater ***(Tamandua tetradactyla)***
Ring-tailed coati ***(Nasua nasua)***
Toco toucan ***(Ramphastos toco)***
Spectacled owl ***(Pulsatrix perspicillata)***
Understorey The upper layers of vegetation prevent much light from reaching the bottom. Here we find orchids, lichens and bracken and many snakes and frogs.
Crimson-crested woodpecker ***(Campephilus menlanoleucus)***
Anteater ***(Myrmeciphaga tridactyla)***
Ground level Less than 2 per cent of the sun's rays reach the ground. It is the habitat of the largest animals as well as thousands of invertebrates.
Collared peccary ***(Pecari tajacu)***

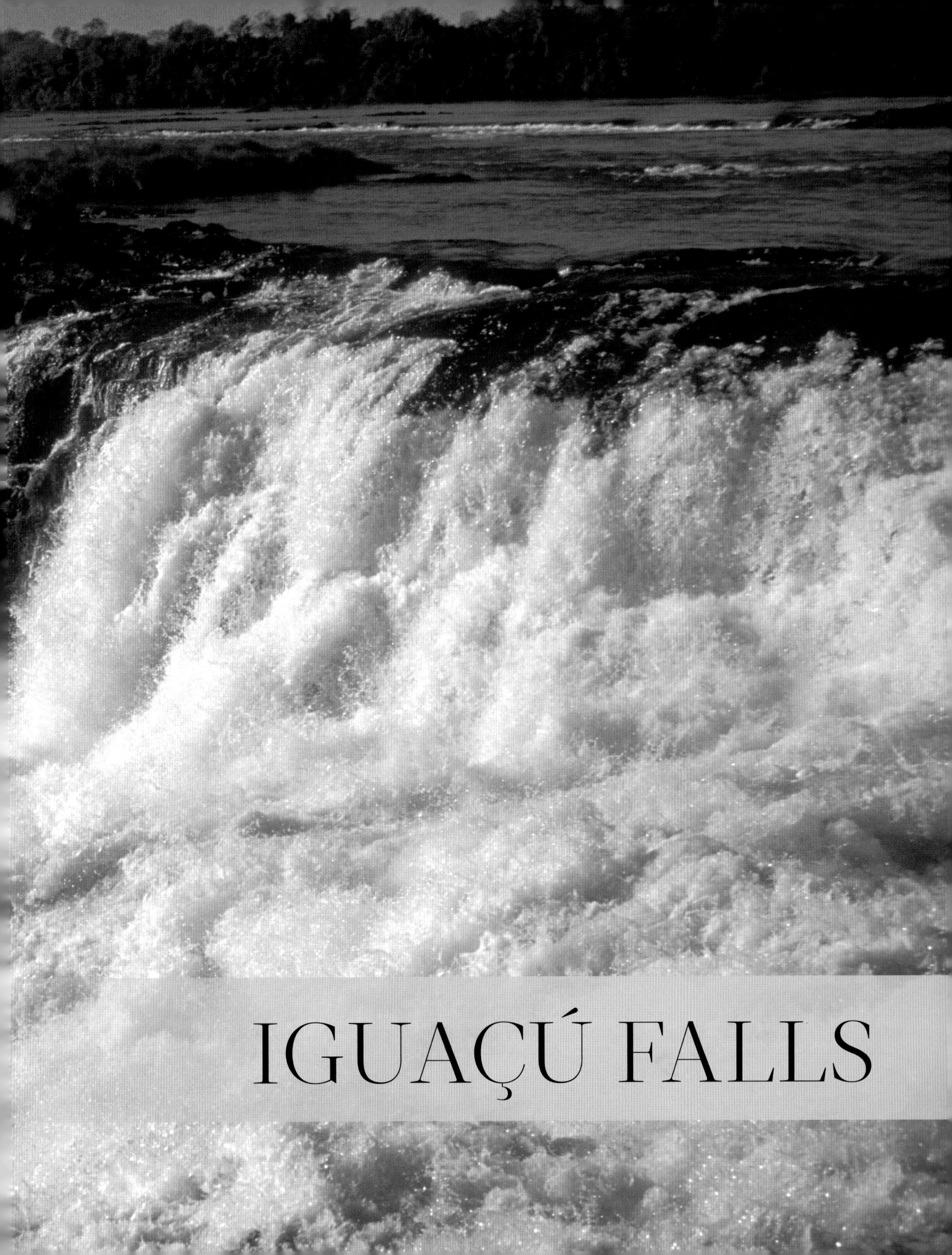

IGUAÇÚ FALLS

Iguaçú Falls Located around the 'Devil's Throat', these waterfalls occupy part of the province of Misiones (Argentina) and the state of Paraná (Brazil), on both sides of the border.

A giant complex of waterfalls

Situated on the border between Argentina, Brazil and Paraguay, the Iguaçú waterfalls demonstrate some of the most powerful displays of the force of water on the planet.

Álvar Núñez Cabeza de Vaca was intimidated by nothing. A 16th-century Andalusian soldier and explorer, he was one of four survivors of a small Spanish fleet shipwrecked opposite the mouth of the Mississippi. During 8 long years, Cabeza de Vaca and his three companions became the first Europeans to explore the Gulf of Mexico and the Pacific coast of the then Viceroyalty of New Spain, on a journey of some 18,000 km (11,185 mi) through North America in search of any town controlled by his native country.

On returning to Spain after his ordeal, which almost cost him his life on numerous occasions, the explorer was unable to adapt to the tranquillity of his Andalusian retirement and asked Emperor Carlos V for a new assignment in the New World, this time as governor of Río de la Plata in the south of the continent where the situation of the Crown's Spanish representatives was more precarious. In 1541, from Santa Catarina Island in Brazil, Cabeza de Vaca began a gruelling five-month journey to Asunción in Paraguay, the seat of the Spanish government headquarters since the fall and subsequent abandonment of Buenos Aires. The expedition crossed mountain ranges, thick forest and large rivers. When they had covered two thirds of a journey of almost 1,000 km (621 mi), in an enclave hidden from the road, the Spanish soldiers began to hear a distant sound which, as they approached the source, became a deafening roar.

140 million tonnes of water every hour

After overcoming the vegetation that hindered their view, Cabeza de Vaca could not avoid displaying intense emotion at the vision of a geological phenomenon which surpassed everything he had experienced in 15 years of American exploration. After being a North American pioneer some years before, he became the first European to stumble upon the awesome Devil's Throat, an 80 m (262 ft) waterfall, over which the Iguaçú River falls with all its might. According to the Andalusian explorer, the din of the water falling over the ravine could be

↑Ecosystem The surrounding environment of the falls comprising subtropical forest with a rich ecosystem is a vision of nature in itself.

heard 25 km (16 mi) away, which is about a seven-hour walk to the edge where the river plunges into the void. When the sun's rays are refracted in the mist caused by the falling water it forms a spectacular rainbow over 100 m (328 ft) wide. Just after the rainy season, in October, 140 million tonnes of water flow every hour over the 275 waterfalls which make up the complete horseshoe of Iguaçú Falls, seven times the volume of the famous Niagara Falls.

As with the latter, situated between Canada and the United States, the Iguaçú Falls are also borders: the river forms the border between Argentina and Brazil, and Paraguay is located just 20 miles downriver at the point where the Iguaçú River flows into the Paraná. Eighty per cent of the falls – arranged in a horseshoe around a deep canyon – are located in Argentina, while it is from Brazil that the best views are obtained. The area where the greatest height and the maximum flow meet is known as the Devil's Throat, at the foot of which is the island of St Martin, accessible by small boats. This allows visitors to get very close to the spectacular waterfalls and, in all likelihood, end up soaking wet.

It was formed in the last million and a half years by erosion from the force of the water on the faults and fractures in the rocks. Several paths offer different options to approach the falls from the top and from the Throat, in order to admire this geological wonder. Another path – the Macuco – allows the visitor to complete the visit with a tour of the humid subtropical forest which surrounds the falls and which, a few decades ago, occupied broad expanses of northern Argentina, southern Brazil and eastern Paraguay.

↑Rainbow On sunny days a large rainbow more than 100 m (328 ft) wide appears.

↗Devil's Throat Aerial view of the Iguazu River's spectacular fall into the deep canyon.

→The force of water The sheer volume of the Iguaçú River falling 80 m (262 ft) causes a deafening roar.

↑Tourism The tourist boats allow visitors to get as close as possible to the waterfalls.

Today, deforestation has left the forest cover greatly reduced. Successful tourism at the falls and their border location – which favours smuggling – has stimulated the growth of cities out of nothing. The city of Foz do Iguaçú on the Brazilian side, which has a population of 250,000 inhabitants, was founded in 1914. On the Argentinian side is Puerto Iguazú, the population of which (85,000 inhabitants) has tripled in the last ten years. And on the Paraguay coast is the Ciudad del Este, with 400,000 registered residents, which was created by government decree in 1957 in order to concentrate the commercial activity of the Paraná River, navigable from the Río de la Plata. These three cities form a unique international metropolitan area, the economic activity of which is based on trans-border trade, harbour activity and tourism generated by the waterfalls.

Although the environment of the falls is still a phenomenal miracle of nature which left Cabeza de Vaca breathless, the way to reach the region today is far from being the dangerous adventure that the intrepid Spanish explorer experienced five centuries ago.

A paradise of biodiversity

Around the falls there are 450 species of bird, 80 species of mammal, countless invertebrates and more than 2,000 species of plant.

Queen palm Common in subtropical forest. It produces inflorescences with white or yellow flowers.

Heart of palm *(Palmito Jucara)* This is one of the palm trees harvested for their delicious hearts of palm.

Jaguar *(Panthera onca)* With a weight between 70 and 130 kg (154 and 287 lbs), it is the largest cat in the Americas, and is also a good swimmer. It is a species in danger of extinction.

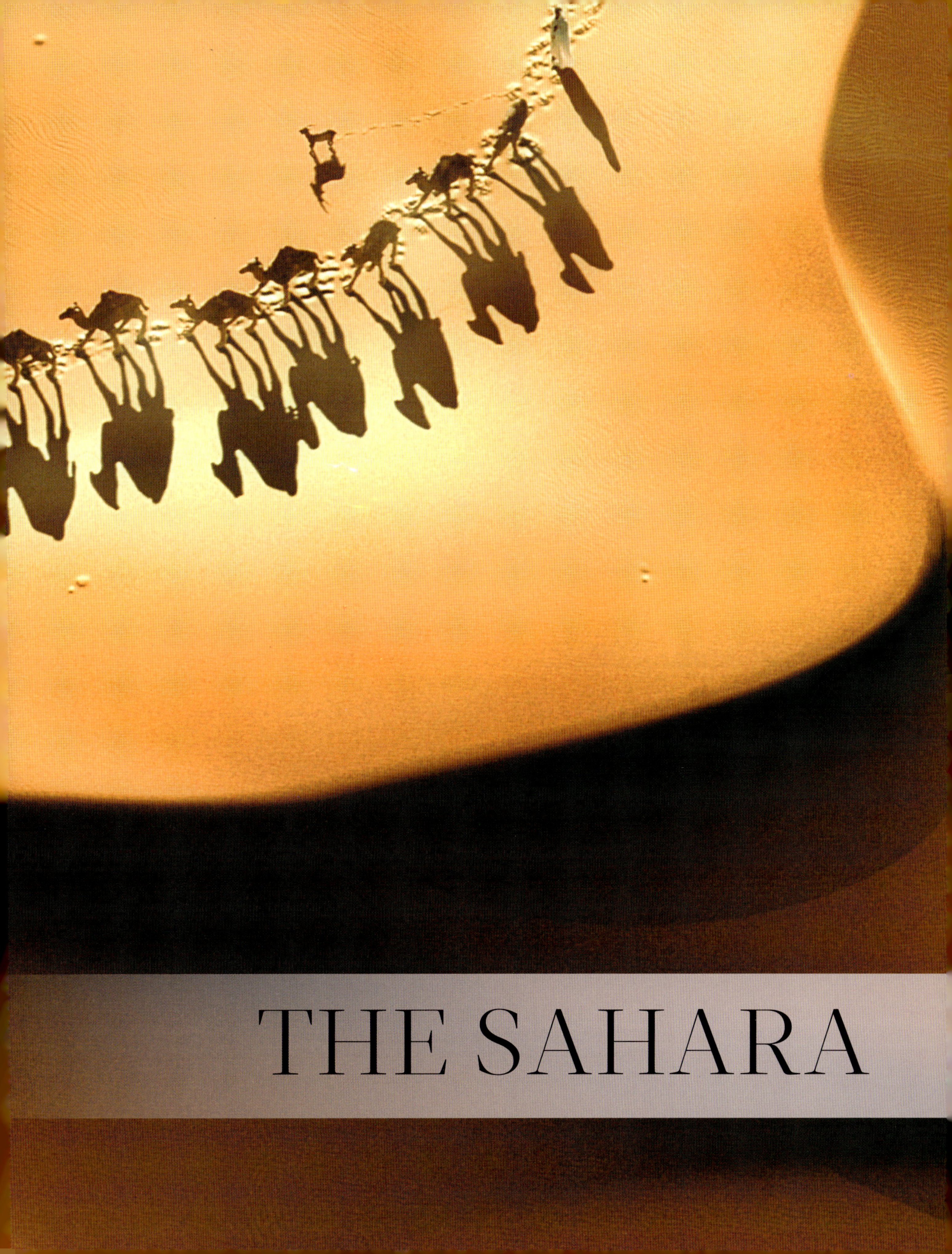

THE SAHARA

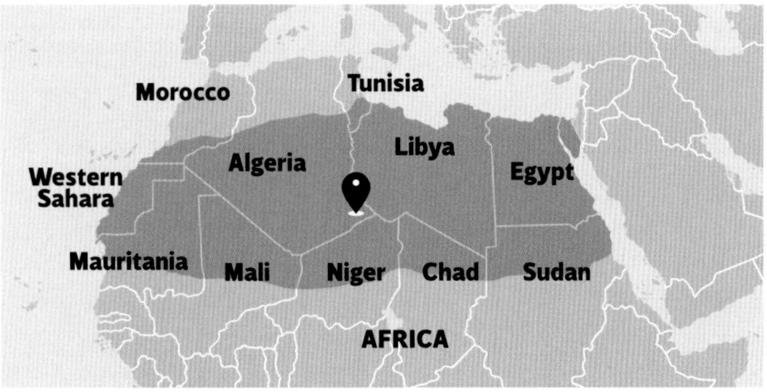

The Sahara Covering an area greater than 9 million km^2 (3.4 million mi^2), this desert covers parts of North Africa, Algeria, Chad, Egypt, Mali, Libya, Morocco, Western Sahara, Mauritania, Niger, Sudan and Tunisia.

More than just sand

The largest desert in the world, the Sahara, occupies much of North Africa. With thousands and thousands of miles of intense heat and aridity, it is a miracle that life can survive there.

A beautiful set of paintings and etchings, found in a shelter on the stony plateau of Tassili n'Ajjer in the south-east of Algeria, shows a group of hunters chasing large herbivores. Drawn around 8,000 years ago, these remarkable artistic North African Neolithic remains confirm the suspicions of many scientists: at that time, very recently in geological terms, the Sahara desert was a savannah with a climate, vegetation and fauna similar to those which today can be found in Kenya and Tanzania. It had multiple permanent water sources in addition to the Nile and a sizeable stable population, considering the low populace of the period, with an important flow of nomadic traders who were very active up until a few hundred years ago.

Today, however, the North African region, which stretches east to west from the Red Sea to the Atlantic coast and north to south from the Mediterranean to the Sahel, is the largest and cruellest desert in the world. Spanning more than 9 million km^2 (3.4 million mi^2), the Sahara is equivalent in size to countries such as the USA, China and Brazil, and covers parts of eleven African states and territories. Its size, unlike a few thousand years ago, has grown in recent decades, partly due to the influence of human activity on the global climate. The Sahel, the border between the desert and the savannah to the south of the Sahara, has, in that time, begun to acquire the characteristics of an arid region, causing subsequent problems for the population, which is forced to migrate to escape hunger and thirst. Some climatologists, however, believe this increase is due to natural oscillations in the ecosystem and warrant that the Sahel is becoming green again with the new millennium.

Geographers consider a desert to be any region where rainfall is less than 250 litres (440 pints) or millimetres (10 inches) per square meter per year: in the centre of the Sahara – the Arabic word meaning desert – there is no more than 25 litres (44 pints) of rainfall every year and there are many regions where the rainfall is less than 5 litres (9 pints). Why is it so extremely dry? The

↑Oasis Palm groves alongside the Um el Ma Lake, in Libya, one of the classic oases which can be found in the desert.

trade winds, caused by air warming up over equatorial regions, are dry currents which blow towards the tropics, dispelling the clouds and allowing the ground to overheat from the constant action of the sun.

Dunes and mountains

Another feature of the Sahara is the torrid heat: on 13 September 1922, El Azizia (Libya) reached a temperature of 56.7° C (134° F), thought to be the highest temperature ever recorded on Earth. Experts believe that areas closest to the heart of the Sahara would have been even hotter, but there were no weather stations to record it. Despite the romantic representation of the Sahara as a sea of sand dunes, the reality is that this erg or sandy desert represents just 20 per cent of the area, while the remainder is the less photogenic reg or hamada or stony desert. In the vast magnitude of the Sahara there is also room for majestic and massive mountain ranges, such as the Atlas Mountains in Morocco and Algeria, which serve as the desert's northern border and reach altitudes of over 4,000 m (13,123 ft), the Ahaggar, in the south of Algeria, almost 3,000 m (9,843 ft), the Tibesti, a volcanic region of Chad over 3,400 m (11,155 ft), and the Aïr Mountains in Niger, reaching heights approaching 2,000 m (6,562 ft).

These climatic and geographical conditions make the Sahara an almost impenetrable barrier placed between the Mediterranean and sub-Saharan Africa, but it was not always so. The Berbers, the indigenous ethnic population of North Africa for at least three millennia, created long trade routes across the desert, especially their nomadic tribes, such as the famous Tuareg. In the Middle Ages, these true desert dwellers were responsible for opening the famous caravan route

↖Timbuktu Located in Mali, for centuries it was a very important city for Saharan trade.

↑Camel caravans These caravans have become a tourist attraction in Saharan countries.

←Desert rose This is an unusual sedimentary rock created in the Sahara, which is formed in the shape of a flower.

←Hamada This type of rocky plateau occupies 80 per cent of the Saharan desert.

across the Sahara, between Marrakesh in southern Morocco, and Timbuktu in Mali, a key Saharan trading city founded by the Tuareg. For almost eight hundred years, well into the 16th century, camel caravans laden with slaves, gold, silver and salt from Central Africa travelled between these two places – a journey of over 2,000 km (1,242 mi).

However, the Tuareg are not the only inhabitants of the Sahara. Despite the harsh climate and lack of food, desert fauna is very diverse, with species such as the dromedary – an artiodactyla whose hump holds a fat deposit which sustains it during food shortages; the fennec or desert fox, with its disproportionately-sized ears, the Addax antelope, Dorcas gazelle, the Lanner falcon and the spiny-tailed lizard. The vegetation, plant species with small leaves to reduce evaporation and deep roots to access underground moisture, is concentrated on the periphery of the desert and in the few palm trees that grow around small seasonal pools, shaded by date palms imported by Arabs in the 7th century.

Survival in the desert

Despite the extreme climate, several species live in the desert, grouped around the few oases.

Nocturnal activity During the day, the oppressive heat forces the majority of animals to take shelter. The sharp drop in temperature at sundown allows them to go out in search of food and water.

VIRUNGA NATIONAL PARK

Virunga The Virunga National Park is in the Great Lakes region of Africa, on Congo's border with Rwanda and Uganda.

A paradise in danger

Gorillas in the Mist, the famous book by American zoologist Dian Fossey, which was later made into a film, tells the story of the author's life in the extraordinary Virunga mountains.

Born in San Francisco in 1932, Dian Fossey was an American zoologist who fell in love with the study of gorillas through the work of two of her teachers: another zoologist, George Schaller, who transmitted his passion for mountain gorillas, and the great archaeologist Louis Leakey, who discovered several ancestors of modern man in Kenya and Tanzania.

In 1963, Fossey took the opportunity to go to Zaire (now the Democratic Republic of the Congo) to observe mountain gorillas close up. This subspecies of the Western gorilla is characterised by longer and thicker fur, a protection that allows them to live on the cold and rugged wooded volcano-sides of the African Great Lakes region, at between 2,200 and 4,200 m (7,200 to 13,800 ft). Active by day and vegetarian, mountain gorillas spend more time on the ground than their cousins from the plains. They feed mainly on gallium vines, a creeper from which they eat the leaves, sprouts, fruit and even flowers, and senecio, a bush which grows in subalpine areas, just under the peaks of the region, which are almost always covered with thick cloud. Stationed in the mountains of Virunga, on the Congo's border with Rwanda and Uganda, Fossey was able to observe the activities and behaviour of the mountain gorillas from very close up, so much so that she managed to gain their confidence enough to become a member of several of their family groups. This almost fraternal affection with the gorillas forced her to confront the factors caused by human activity that were leading to a rapid decline in their populations: poaching, the wars that have scourged the area in recent years, contagion with human-borne diseases, since the two species are genetically very similar, and the serious damage to the habitat of these extraordinary primates, victim of intense deforestation during much of the 20th century.

The zoologist made herself such a thorn in the side of the gangs of poachers that she had to cross the border from the Congo and set up again in Rwanda, and finally, in 1985, she was murdered by machete in her camp, a few days after her 54th birthday.

↑Nyiragongo This stratovolcano in the Virunga mountains is one of the most active in Africa.

After Fossey's death, the atmosphere of constant civil war on the border region of Virunga since 1997 has aggravated the traditional lack of protection of the local fauna: during this period many militant groups have dedicated themselves to the systematic extermination of animals in danger of extinction, with the simple aim of capturing the attention of the international community, which often cares more about attacks on the natural heritage than on the regional civilian population.

Large protected area

Today, the day-to-day work of technicians in the Virunga National Park is a tribute to the legacy of Dian Fossey. Created in 1925, it was one of the first protected areas created on the African continent, and its extraordinary fauna is very much threatened by poachers. Currently only 700 individual mountain gorillas survive, compared with 16,000 of the plains variety. The forest elephant – a smaller species than the African elephants that live in the savannah – is also in a critical situation, as is the hippopotamus: poaching has killed 95 per cent of the individuals that lived on the shores of Lake Edward in the north of the park. Virunga also shelters notable populations of chimpanzees, giraffes, buffalo and okapi.

The Virunga mountains form a branch of the so-called Albertina Fault, an offshoot of the Great Rift Valley, the colossal geological break that crosses Africa from north to south, generating intense volcanic activity. Located between Lake Edward and Lake Kivu, in the Great Lakes region, this mountain range includes eight volcanoes, two of which are among the most active of the planet: Nyiragongo, at 3,470 m (11,380 ft), whose last eruption in 2002 destroyed the nearby locality of Gomo, and Nyamuragira, at 3,063 m (10,050 ft), which became

↑Elephants They live in the savannah of the mountainsides.

↗Lava lake The crater of Nyiragongo's volcano holds the largest lava lake in the world.

→The forests The dominant species in the forests of Virunga is the hagenia.

↑Mountain gorillas One of the most threatened species on the planet.

volcanically active in 2010, creating yet another threat to the region's fauna. Mount Karisimbi is the highest mountain in the park at 4,507 m (14,800 ft). It is located on the Congo/Rwanda border and on its slopes there stands the Karisoke Research Centre, which was founded by Fossey in 1967.

But not all the park (of a total of 7,800 km² [3,012 mi²]) has the mountainous relief of wooded slopes that the gorillas need. The protected area also includes large areas of marshland adjoining lakes Edward and Kivu, plains and transition grasslands, large lava fields in the skirts of the volcanoes, mountain pastures in the subalpine zone, and on the peak of Karisimbi, one of the last glaciers in Africa still survives global warming. The Virunga park forms a cross-border continuum with another two protected areas: the Volcanoes National Park, in Rwanda, which includes the eastern side of the Virunga mountains, and the impenetrable forest of Bwindi, in Uganda, one of the richest and most virgin ecosystems of the African continent, with exceptional biodiversity.

The land of the gorillas

The forests of the Virunga National Park are the habitat of one of the most threatened species on the planet, the mountain gorillas.

Glacier The highest peaks are above 4,000 m (13,000 ft) and have perpetual snow.

Undergrowth The thick branches of the hagenia tree, covered in lichen and moss, allow light to reach the ground, where the vegetation is very thick.

Mountain gorilla *(Gorilla beringei beringei)* In the undergrowth, the gorillas find their food, a diet based on roots, shoots, leaves, flowers and fruit. They complement this vegetable diet by eating insects, larvae and snails.

Okapi *(Okapia johnstoni)* This is a species endemic to the Congo.

Hagenia *(Hagenia abyssinica)*
A slender tree that can reach 20 m (66 ft) in height and the dominant species in the forest where the gorillas live.
Oberläender's ground thrush *(Zoothera oberlaenderi)*
Communication
The gorillas make about 25 different sounds, which they use to indicate the location of the members of the group and to impose discipline.
Nuhan's Francolin *(Francolinus nahani)*

KILIMANJARO

Kilimanjaro This colossus of 5,892 m (19,331 ft), the highest point in Africa, is located in the north-east of Tanzania and forms part of the nature park named after it.

The high point of Africa

6 km (4 mi) above sea level and almost 5 km (3 mi) above its own base, Mount Kilimanjaro is the king of the African savannah, over which it presides with power and grandeur.

Unlike what happens with the high points of other continents, half hidden among neighbouring giants in large mountain ranges like the Himalayas, the Andes, the Caucasus or the Rockies, the roof of Africa is an enormous volcano which stands in the middle of the savannah, visible on clear days from several hundred kilometres all around. This privileged position, its tremendous size and the perpetual snow that covers its peak have made Kilimanjaro the sacred mountain for the Maasai and the Chagga, the ethnic groups that have inhabited the region since time immemorial.

Kilimanjaro is, in fact, an enormous volcanic mountain made up of three aligned cones: Shira, to the west, is 3,962 m (13,000 ft) high; Mawenzi, to the east, reaches 5,149 m (16,900 ft); and Kibo, in the centre, is the highest of the three at 5,892 m (19,330 ft), and forms the overall peak, known as Uhuru and was climbed for the first time in 1889. Its name in Swahili (Kilima Ndjaro) and in Maasai (Ol Doinyo Oibor) mean 'Shining Mountain' or 'White Mountain' because of the snow cover at the top.

Unfortunately, the glaciers that surround the crater of Kibo, once magnificent rivers of snow that reflected the intense light of the equatorial sun like mirrors, are now feeble victims of climate change.

The mountain is located in the north of Tanzania, a few kilometres from the frontier with Kenya. Located as it is in the middle of the plain of the African savannah, on a table a few thousand metres high, Kilimanjaro can be considered the highest isolated peak in the world, as it rises some 4,800 m (15,750 ft) from its base, which is the same as Mont Blanc from sea level. Kibo, the youngest and most elevated volcano of the group, forms an enormous basin which holds the principal crater, almost one kilometre (0.62 mi) across inside. The mountain, located on the westernmost fault of the Great Rift Valley, which is one of the deepest and most active geological faults in the Earth, was formed some 2.5 million years ago. The Shira volcano, on the western side of Kilimanjaro, dates from that period. Later on, Mawenzi, the easternmost volcano, erupted, and after that Kibo,

↑Heath zone In this stratum of Kilimanjaro, the predominant vegetation is heathland and brush.

which became active 600,000 years ago and has held a lava lake in its crater for just 5,000 years. Today it is considered inactive, even though from time to time its fumaroles release gas into the air, which make its seismic shifts easily perceptible.

From savannah to glaciers

The geographical isolation is one of the characteristics that make Kilimanjaro so unique, making it easy to identify the bands of vegetation according to altitude and orientation. At its lowest point are the plains or lowlands, situated between 800 and 1,600 m (2,600 and 5,200 ft) and with a hot, dry climate. In this typical savannah environment, the vegetation is primarily grassland, with isolated acacias and baobabs. The mountain stratum, between 1,600 and 2,700 m (5,200 and 8,900 ft) is filled with tropical forest, which makes a belt of dense vegetation between the savannah base and the alpine zone. This band is subdivided into various well differentiated ecosystems: the dry forest – now very deteriorated; the rainforest – home to the leopard, the cerval and several species of primates; and the cloud forest – whose trees are totally covered in moss and ferns and nourished by the dew that rises from the rainforest where abundant fog in the higher parts condenses into rain.

In the so-called heath zone, between 2,800 and 4,000 m (9,200 and 13,125 ft), the vegetation thins out and very occasionally you can see large mammals like lions, buffalos, leopards or hyenas, which prefer to come up to these altitudes before crossing the mountain as they move from one side of the plain to the other. Even higher, between 4,000 and 5,000 m (13,125 and 16,400 ft), there is the Afro-alpine zone, characterised by a cold, dry climate, something that leads to a radical reduction of plant

↑Erosion In some areas the action of water has marked blue and white bands on the rocks.

↗Glaciers According to specialists, their days are numbered. In less than a century their surface area has gone from 12 to 2 km^2 (4.6 to 0.8 mi^2).

↗Maasai This african tribe lives off herding at the foot of Kilimanjaro.

→The Reusch Crater This is the central crater of Kibo, the mountain's highest volcanic cone.

diversity, as only species that are capable of adapting to the prevailing rigorous climate survive. Finally, between 5,000 m (16,400 ft) and the summit there is the snow area, with terrain consisting of rock and ice, where there is almost no life.

All these layers have been protected since 1973 by the declaration of a national park, even though this measure has not succeeded in slowing the degradation that Kilimanjaro has undergone since the beginning of the 20th century. The progressive melting of the glaciers due to global warming has added to the deforestation of the forest in the mountain stratum, caused by the activity of the tribes living in the region. The north and west of the volcano are occupied by the Maasai, a pastoral people, one of whose most ancient traditions is to start controlled fires to regenerate the earth with the carbonised vegetation. The south and the east, on the other hand, are occupied by Chagga peasants, who tend to extend their fields right up to the slopes of Kilimanjaro, despite awareness campaigns by park authorities.

Three large volcanoes in one

Kilimanjaro has three large craters – Kibo, Mawenzi and Shira – although they have not been active for more than 100,000 years.

Under protection The Kilimanjaro National Park occupies an area of 75,353 hectares (186,201 acres) and includes both the volcano and the mountain forests and part of the savannah that surrounds it.

Environments Due to its altitude, Kilimanjaro has different environments with their own characteristics.

- Snow environment
- Afro-alpine environment
- Mattoral, plain and scrub
- Cloud forest
- Rainforest
- Savannah and plantations

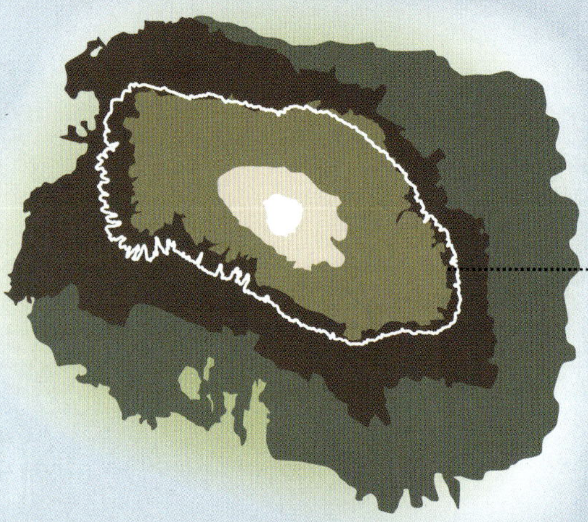

Shira cone The oldest and most eroded of the three cones of Kilimanjaro, it measures 3,962 m (13,000 ft).

Glaciers in retreat If the current tendency, provoked by global warming, continues, the mountain may lose all its glaciers before 2030.

Fauna On the surrounding plains there are large mammals such as lions, zebras and elephants.

Not so alone In reality, Kilimanjaro forms part of a chain of volcanoes located on the eastern margin of the Great Rift Valley.

Cone of Kibo This is the youngest of the cones. Its profile is surrounded by gentle slopes. It still releases volcanic gases.

The saddle This valley, located between the cones of Kibo and Mawenzi, is located at about 3,600 m (11,800 ft) above sea level, and contains the largest area of mountain tundra vegetation in Africa.

Breach wall This is a wall that borders a deep fissure in the mountain, the product of an ancient landslide.

Mawenzi cone At 5,149 m (16,900 ft) it is the third highest peak in Africa. Although it is only 6 km (3.7 mi) away from the cone of Kibo, it is completely different, with a scarped, abrupt profile.

ANJAJAVY

Anjajavy Forest Located in the west of the Island of Madagascar, in the middle of the Indian Ocean, Anjajavy Forest is separated from the African continent by the Strait of Mozambique.

A unique natural refuge

Madagascar conceals one of the most extraordinary habitats of the world: the *tsingy*, a calcareous rock formation that has become a paradise for lemurs.

Located some 400 km to the east of Africa, in the Indian Ocean, Madagascar is the fourth largest island on the planet, with a surface area bigger than France. Its geological history is eventful: at first it formed part of the supercontinent Gondwana, which joined in a single gigantic block the land that today makes up South America, Africa, India, the Antarctic and Australia. 140 million years ago, these three last regions, including Madagascar, began a slow but definite journey to the East, separating themselves from Africa and South America. And 80 million years ago, the island separated from India, which continued to move and today lies some 2,000 km (1,240 mi) to the north–east.

What is the point of these geology lessons? Without them, we would not understand the real uniqueness of Madagascar, an island near Africa but more closely related to India, something that non–experts easily realise, but holds specialists particularly enthralled when studying its wildlife, its vegetation and its rock formations. In fact, the island shows the adaptation and evolution of many species after these 80 million years of isolation from others with a common origin today that live in Asia and Africa. This process has encouraged a very high degree of endemism, that is, a very high number of families or species of animals and plants that are only found in Madagascar, a fact that makes the Big Red Island – as it is known because of the characteristic colour of its soil – into a real paradise for biologists.

The curious 'tsingys'

Much of the surface of Madagascar is dominated by a central plain that descends abruptly towards the East, where it forms a narrow coastal strip of wet tropical forest, and towards the West, where the climate becomes drier and deciduous woodland starts. The forest of Anjajavy, located on the north–east of the island, is located in this latter region. It covers just 50 km² (19.3 mi²) of a small peninsula that projects into the Mozambique Channel, near a town of the same name, and holds some strange geological formations – the so–called *tsingys* – characteristic of the west of the island and which are

↑Red tsingy Due to deforestation, the red *tsingys* have appeared in the last 50 years.

↗Unique With their extraordinary shapes, these rocks are also known as 'forests of stone'.

responsible, due to their harsh, inaccessible relief, for the relatively good state of conservation; the area being much better preserved than other ecological jewels which have suffered so badly in Madagascar. The *tsingys* are limestone outcrops, eroded by the abundant rains of the region. The process has formed large areas of very thin pinnacles, practically impossible for human beings to cross, which has meant they have become havens for curious native species, such as the extraordinary fossa, which is the largest carnivore of the island, related to the mongoose and the civet, but looking more like a cat or dog, and several endemic species of chameleon, a family of which half the known species are housed by Madagascar. Also, a few tens of metres under the *tsingys*, in the caves created by the same erosion of water acting on limestone, there are mysterious underground rivers inhabited by eels, crocodiles and several species of bats.

However, the real symbols of the park and all the island's fauna are the lemurs, so-called because their cries, nocturnal habits and round, shining eyes reminded the first Europeans who studied them of the mythological lemurs, the spectres that according to the Romans came out of graves to attack the living. The ancestors of these primates reached Madagascar 50 million years ago, probably on tree trunks floating from the African coast, and once on the island evolved with little competition, until they had diversified to more than a hundred different species.

When man reached Madagascar, between 2,300 and 1,600 years ago, there were lemurs the size of gorillas, but nowadays many species have died out. Among the survivors, many of which are in danger of extinction,

↑Chameleon Arboreal chameleons have prehensile claws that allow them to cling to rough surfaces.

↗A leap The lemur uses its tail, which is not prehensile, to balance its weight when it jumps.

↑Tenrec Of the 30 known families of tenrecs – the Tenrecidae – most are endemic to Madagascar.

↗Fossa Another endemic species is the fossa – *Cryptoprocta ferox* – a carnivore from the Eupleridae family.

→Baobabs The Grandieri baobab – *Adansonia grandieri*, to give it its scientific name – is the largest of the six species living in Madagascar.

there is still huge diversity: there are lemurs from 30 g to 9 kg. Even so, they all share some common characteristics: they have five-fingered hands and feet with opposing thumbs – a feature that characterises most primates, including humans – with fingernails rather than claws, a hairless nose and a varied diet of fruit and leaves.

Beyond the peculiar habitat of the *tsingy*, Anjajavy offers extensive areas of deciduous forest, with tree species from 15 to 30 m (50 to 100 ft) tall, like the spectacular baobabs, which accumulate large quantities of water in their large bulbous trunks in order to survive the dry season, from May to September. Unlike the *tsingy* areas, these forest areas are in a bad state of conservation because of the practice of subsistence farming by the local population. That said, the degradation here is not comparable to that suffered by the forests in the central and eastern zones, where human pressure is much greater. In the case of Anjajavy, water scarcity and regional communications deficiencies work in favour of the conservation of the ecosystem.

Life in the forest

This large dry tropical forest has many endemic species, like lemurs or chameleons, and the countryside has majestic baobabs.

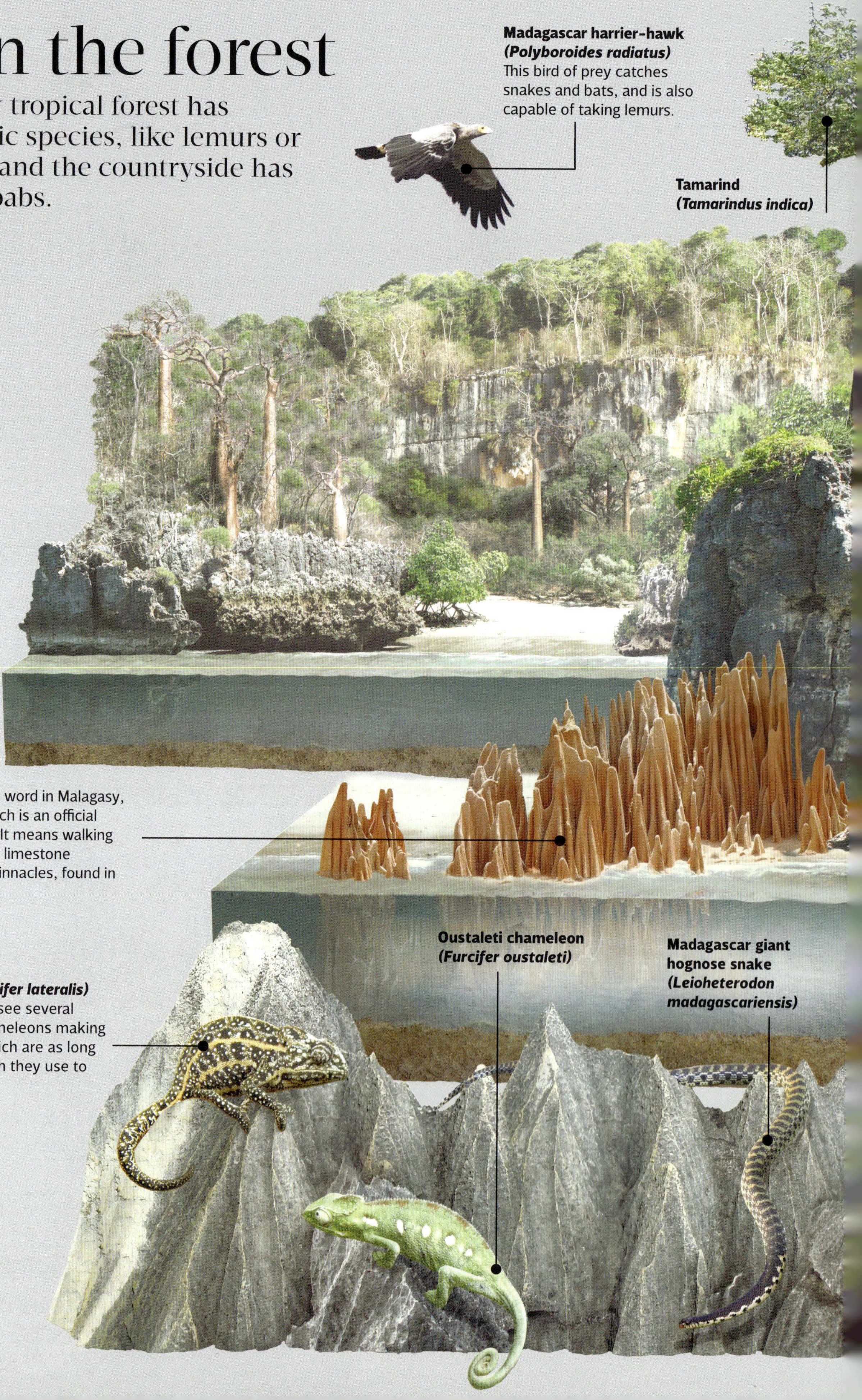

Madagascar harrier-hawk *(Polyboroides radiatus)* This bird of prey catches snakes and bats, and is also capable of taking lemurs.

Tamarind *(Tamarindus indica)*

Stone needles *Tsingy* is a word in Malagasy, which together with French is an official language in Madagascar. It means walking on tiptoe. The *tsingys* are limestone outcrops in the form of pinnacles, found in forests and in the sea.

Carpet chameleon *(Furcifer lateralis)* In the *tsingys* you often see several endemic species of chameleons making use of their tongues, which are as long as their bodies and which they use to catch insects for food.

Oustaleti chameleon *(Furcifer oustaleti)*

Madagascar giant hognose snake *(Leioheterodon madagascariensis)*

Baobab (*Adansonia rubrostipa*)

Common brown lemur (*Eulemur fulvus*) These ancient primates are as happy climbing trees as they are on the ground. They eat flowers, fruit and leaves. Anjajavy includes species like the Coquerel's Sifaka, the common brown lemur and the Milne-Edwards' sportive lemur.

Madagascar ground boa (*Acratophis madagascariensis*)

Leaf-nosed bat The interior of the *tsingys* offer refuge to bats, especially the leaf-nosed varieties.

Western girdled lizard (*Zonosaurus laticaudatus*)

Fossa (*Cryptoprocta ferox*) This mammal, endemic to the island, measures 80–90 cm (30–35 in) and can weigh as much as 10 kg (22 lbs). Extremely agile and fast-moving, it is the lemurs' primary predator.

THE HIMALAYAS

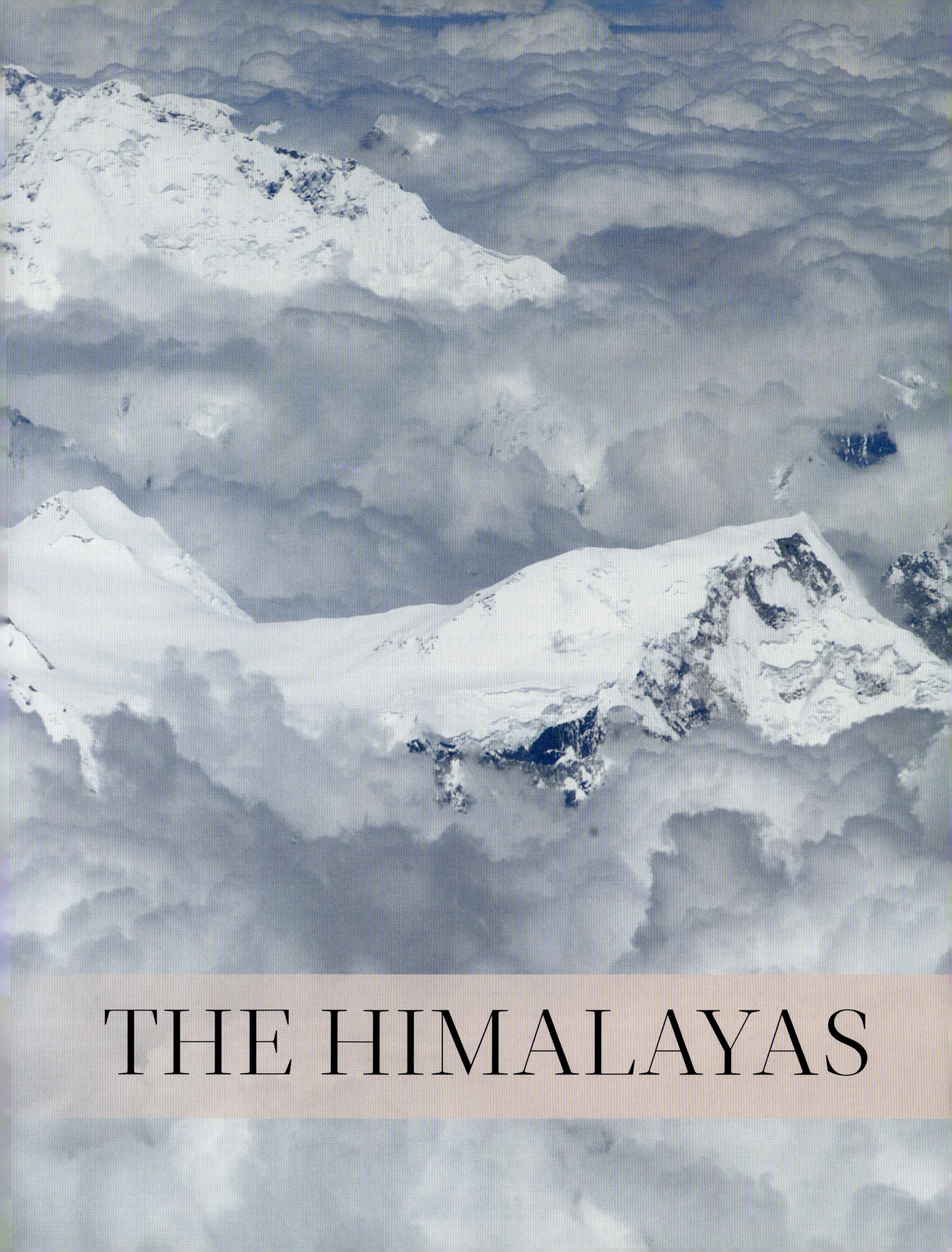

The Himalayas The Himalayan mountain range, shared by India, Pakistan, Nepal, China and Bhutan in the south of Asia, has the world's highest mountains.

The roof of the world

With peaks exceeding 8,000 m (26,000 ft), the highest mountain range in the world is an almost impassable barrier between the Indian subcontinent and the rest of Asia.

Take a piece of paper. Lay it horizontally on a table. Pick up the ends of the paper and press them until they meet in the middle. What has happened? The paper has made a wave which lifted several centimetres off the table. Now try and imagine this happening at a planetary scale. Even if our eyes wouldn't have been able to see it, in the south of Asia, two enormous tectonic plates took millions of years to smash brutally against each other, at a velocity of just a few centimetres per year. In this case, the forces are not those of your hands pressing on the table but, on one side, the colossal Eurasiatic Plate, and on the other, the no less powerful Indo-Australian Plate. But the result, on a different scale, is similar: the few centimetres that the paper lifted off the table translate on Earth to the 8,848 m (29,029 ft) of Mount Everest, the highest peak on the planet, and the focal point of the enormous mountain range raised by the constant pressure of these two plates: the Himalayas. The numbers are convincing: the Himalayas have nine of the ten highest peaks in the world and ten of the 14 'eight-thousanders', a name given by climbers to mountains above 8,000 m (5 mi), the altitude at which the so-called 'death zone' begins. A climber's challenges are many: the extremely low air pressure reduces breathable oxygen to one third; the temperatures are so low that the extremities are constantly threatened by frostbite, and consequently by almost certain amputation; the winds reach 140 km per hour (86 mph) and any slip, whether caused by fatigue, altitude sickness, the technical difficulties of the ascent or the extreme slipperiness of the ice, can lead to a fall of several hundred metres.

An extraordinary mountain range

The ancestral home of several ethnic groups, among whom include the Sherpas, who are used to acting as guides for mountaineering expeditions, the Himalayas became known in the West through the conquest of India by the British Empire and the efforts of great 19th-century British geographers and topographers, who realised they were facing a mountain range of extraordinary dimensions. Mount Everest itself, named Chomolungma or Sagarmatha by the local people,

↑Far from the snow Agriculture has flourished on the gentle green hills of the Himalayas for hundreds of years.

bears the name of the Welsh geographer George Everest, who was responsible for the topography of India and Nepal between 1830 and 1843.

With such altitudes, the Himalayas is a natural border region spanning five countries: India, Pakistan, Nepal, Bhutan and China. This means that many of the main peaks have international approaches: Everest, Lhotse, Makalu and Cho Oyu, for example, can be reached from the Chinese side or the Nepali side. Almost all the great rivers of south Asia have their sources in the lakes and springs of the Himalayas: the Indus has its source on the eastern side of the range and flows into the Arabian Sea, while the Ganges and the Brahmaputra also rise on the northern side, but release their waters into the Gulf of Bengal in the Indian Ocean. The Irrawaddy, Burma's great river, rises on the eastern side of the Himalayas and flows into the Andaman Sea, also in the Indian Ocean.

Reach the summit

The European fever for exploring these majestic and exotic mountains started at the beginning of the 20th century, and since then has given rise to epic stories that could fill entire chapters in the history of human audacity. For example, there is the case of the British climber George Mallory (1886–1924), whose corpse was found 500 m (1,600 ft) from the summit of Everest, with no way of knowing whether or not he had reached his objective. If he managed it, he got there 29 years before the first human beings to have officially reached the roof of the world, in 1953: New Zealander Edmund Hillary and Nepalese Sherpa Tensing Norgay. Three years previously, in 1950, the extremely dangerous Annapurna had become the first of the 'eight-thousanders' to be climbed by human beings: the Frenchmen Maurice Herzog and Louis Lachenal, who paid the price of all

↑Key Gompa This Tibetan monastery in the Spiti valley is at an altitude of more than 4,000 m (13,000 ft).

↗From green land to snow The hills and valleys give way to enormous, arid white mountains.

→Difficulties With its harsh terrain and its lack of infrastructure, donkeys are still used for transport in the Himalayas.

↑Thyme The flowers of Himalayan thyme are used in traditional medicine.

their toes for the victory (and for Herzog, his fingers too). The epic feat of Austrian mountaineer Heinrich Harrer, author of the book *Seven Years in Tibet*, which was made a film in 1997, is also a momentous point in history. As is the achievement of the Sherpa Pemba Dorjie, who participated in a Belgian expedition and became the fastest person to have reached the Everest Summit without additional oxygen, on May 23 2003. Dorjie started out from the base camp at 5,350 m (17,553 ft) and reached the summit at 8,850 m (29,035 ft) in 12 hours and 45 minutes.

Today, more than half a century after those great deeds, the Himalayas are the aim of every self-respecting professional climber. The base camp of Mount Everest, a paradigm of the commercialisation of high mountains, has lost most of the epic flavour of former times, and has become a veritable rubbish dump, in which thousands of professional and amateur expeditions have dumped their trash without any control, with no regard for the virginal beauty of one of the last frontiers of the Earth.

At the foot of the mountains

The Himalayas are a very hostile environment for animals. However, the differences in temperature and air quality do allow several species to survive.

Strata Herbs, moss, lichens and small shrubs can grow up to 4,500 m (14,750 ft). Up to 3,500 m (11,500 ft), there are forests of Himalayan pine, cedar, birch and juniper.

Insects In the high places, plants attract thousands of insects, and this in turn attracts many birds in search of food.

Rhesus monkey (*Macaca mulatta*)
Peregrine falcon (*Falco peregrinus*)
Himalayan griffon vulture (*Gyps himalayensis*)
Asiatic brown bear *(Ursus thibetanus)* It can spend half its time in trees. It is hunted, especially for its bile duct, which is used in Asian cooking and also in various medicines.
Himalayan serow (*Capricornis thar*)
Yak *(Bos grunniens)* The flesh of the yak is as tender as beef but richer in nutrients, and yak milk has fed the Tibetans for millennia.

NIAGARA FALLS

Canada and the United States of America The River Niagara marks the border between the two countries, with one of the falls, the largest, in Canada, and the other two in the United States.

Glorious water

The differences in water level between the North American Great Lakes create marvels like Niagara Falls, which has become one of the classic natural attractions of the continent.

The Niagara is an unusual river: it has a course of only 40 km (24.8 mi), which is the distance between Lakes Erie and Ontario, the two smallest lakes of the enormous Great Lakes system, the world's largest fresh water surface in a liquid state. In this very short course, the Niagara forms the border between the United States and Canada and carries a large volume that has to overcome a considerable difference in level, 107 m (340 ft), half of which is done in one go in the famous falls, nearly one kilometre (3,280 ft) wide, over which some 168,000 m^3 (6 million ft^3) of water surge every minute (in the period of greatest flow).

The Iroquois Algonquin Indians, the inhabitants of the region before the coming of the French and English colonists, called these falls *Oniákara*, which means 'thundering water' in Iroquois. The Europeans first heard about this spectacular natural wonder from the Indians themselves, who believed that the spirit of the falls had the right to demand a human sacrifice every year. Based on these histories and legends, in 1657 the name of Niagara was included for the first time on a French map, and two decades later, two explorers – Frenchman René-Robert Cavelier de La Salle and Belgian Louis Hennepin – became the first Europeans to witness this natural wonder.

But what caused the enormous difference in level, over which the River Niagara falls? During the last Ice Age – which took place between 110,000 and 10,000 years ago – all the territory of today's Canada, with a good part of what is now the United States, was completely covered with a colossal sheet of ice, similar to what now covers Greenland or the Antarctic. The waters produced by the melting of this enormous mass of ice made a sea that was at first connected with the Gulf of Mexico, and then later with the Atlantic Ocean, but ended up as an inland sea. The Great Lakes are what is left from this great mass of water, which was originally glacial. Its current relief explains this obstruction: an elevation of the land separated Lake Ontario, the closest to the Atlantic, from the other lakes of the

↑**Goat Island** Goat Island divides the falls into two parts: Shoshone (United States) and Horseshoe (Canada).

system. This movement left the four higher lakes with no means of emptying, and this created enormous water pressure at one end of Lake Erie. Century after century, millennium after millennium, the pressure from all this water pushed a way through the limestone – a stone that erodes easily – until it made a natural channel, the River Niagara, to connect lakes Erie and Ontario.

Progressive displacement

In the first periods of existence of the River Niagara, the falls were very close to Lake Ontario. Since then, the force of the river has made the falls move back to their current location, at a speed of about one metre per year, and in the future they will move closer and closer to the source Lake Erie. Today, as the river leaves Lake Erie, it flows calmly in a wide stream measuring more than one kilometre (3,300 ft). A little before the halfway point in its course, the Niagara divides into two branches, forming an island in the middle. A few kilometres before the falls, the branches unite again and the river meets the drop with renewed force. Two thirds of the width of the falls are in Canadian territory, where the drop is approximately 52 m (160 ft) and one third is inside the United States, with a maximum drop of 55 m (169 ft). Between the beautiful horseshoe made by the Canadian section and the US part of the cataracts, the Shoshone Falls, is Goat Island, an uninhabited piece of land now accessible by bridges, which offers visitors some of the most spectacular views of the falls.

Under the falls, the water forms a calm pool with surprising speed. This allows the boats of the Maid of the Mist company, to go as close as they can to the spray made by the pulverised water after its violent fall, under a rainbow that is always there when the sun is

↑'Behind the falls' One of the tours for visitors gives you access to an amazing viewpoint next to the waterfall.

↗Spanish Aerocar This picturesque cable car crosses the Whirlpool area.

→Horseshoe The spectacular aerial view of the Canadian part of the falls explains the reason for its name.

↑Maid of the Mist These boats bring tourists right up to the area where the cascades fall.

out. Another option to approach the falls is to try the so-called Spanish Aerocar: a cable car designed by a Spanish engineer in 1916 and still in service that takes tourists across a part of the Canadian sector. Those preferring wider perspectives can climb up one of the viewing towers built next to the natural attraction: the Skylon Tower and the Konica Minolta Tower.

In fact, in the last century the surroundings of the falls have become completely built up. Two towns with the same name – the not very imaginative Niagara Falls – stand on either side of the river: the town on the United States side was founded in 1892 and has 56,000 inhabitants, while the Canadian Niagara Falls is a bit bigger (83,000 residents) and was founded eleven years later. The attraction of the famous falls has called the attention of intrepid adventurers, like Annie Edson Taylor, the woman who in 1901 survived going over the falls in a wooden barrel, or the French tightrope artist Jean François Gravelet, who crossed the 340 m (1,115 ft) width of the falls on a cable 8 cm (3 in) thick.

A great tourist complex

A large change of level along the course of the River Niagara, half way between Lakes Erie and Ontario has created this great wonder of nature.

Observation tower This platform, with its unfinished bridge structure, offers a beautiful view of the falls on the US side. At its base stands the departure point for the Maid of the Mist, the boat that approaches the area where the cascades fall.

Maid of the Mist This is the spot on the Canadian side where the boats leave for the trip to the foot of the Horseshoe Falls.

Shoshone Falls Approximately 323 m wide and 55 m high. Next to it, separated by Moon Island, is the small Bridal Veil Falls. Both are in the State of New York.

Pedestrian walkway A lift takes visitors to the base of the American side of the falls, where there is a path made up of wooden platforms and catwalks leading to the Cave of the Winds, under the Bridal Veil Waterfall.

Whirpool aerocar Almost one hundred years old, this peculiar cable car, with room for 35 people, crosses the River Niagara over a beautiful whirlpool that forms in a stretch of water behind the falls.

Goat Island

Horseshoe Falls Its width of 792 m (2,600 ft) and its attractive horseshoe shape make it into the largest and most spectacular of the three waterfalls of Niagara. Over 90 per cent of the river's flow passes over it.

ainbow Bridge Rainbow Bridge crosses the iver Niagara, joining the two towns called iagara Falls, the one in Canada and the one in ıe USA. That means it is a frontier post, with ıe corresponding customs facilities.

HE GRAND CANYON

The Grand Canyon This geological marvel follows the course of the Colorado River in Arizona (United States of America), over 446 km (277 mi) and forms part of the Colorado National Park.

The force of erosion

The Grand Canyon is not only one of the largest landscapes on Earth, it is an open book that demonstrates planet Earth's geological history.

'Suddenly the ground fell away from my feet. I looked down and saw an abyss so deep and so magnificent I lacked words to describe it.' These were the first impressions of Spanish soldier and explorer García López de Cárdenas, in 1542, on finding himself in front of this massive ravine that nature had patiently created over the last five million years. López de Cárdenas, the first European to discover the Grand Canyon of Colorado, was part of a Spanish expedition searching for the Seven Cities of Gold of Cibola, a legend which originated in Spain in the 8th century when the Iberian Peninsula fell into Muslim hands. The gold of this mythical land was never found, but the expedition helped them to discover one of the most extraordinary marvels on the planet.

However, the history of the Grand Canyon began many years before. Some 70 million years ago, at the end of the Cretaceous period, began the oregeny, a mountain formation process which formed the Rocky Mountains, when various plates pushed under the North American plate, and caused a slow but certain increase in the height of the Colorado plateau, which occupies a large part of the actual states of Arizona, New Mexico, Utah and Colorado, reaching 3,000 m (9,843 ft) high. The formation of the Grand Canyon did not begin until 5.3 million years ago, when the erosive action of the Colorado River on the plains of the plateau was stimulated by the formation of the Gulf of California at its mouth. One million years ago, the depth of the canyon was already the same as it is today: a vertical drop of 1,500 m (4,921 ft) which leaves visitors to the region open-mouthed. The Petronas Towers of Kuala Lumpur could fit inside it three times over, one on top of the other, and there would still be room to spare.

But the Grand Canyon's value is not due just to its extraordinary dimensions, nor to its gigantic rocky landscape which takes on a thousand different shades at sunset, nor even the silvery reflections emanating from the Colorado River, clearly visible from the top: during the patient task of erosion, the river has exposed for all to see, almost half of the geological history of Earth,

↑Horseshoe curve This formidable bend, close to the city of Page, is one of the most visited sections of the Grand Canyon.

from the Precambrian to the Cenozoic eras. The water has cut through the layers of sediment which were deposited in the region many years before the Colorado plateau lifted up and the Rocky Mountains were formed. In fact, 1.8 billion years ago – the age of the oldest stones at the bottom of the canyon – the planet was very different to the one we inhabit today: oxygen had barely begun to accumulate in the atmosphere, the first complex single-cell life forms had just begun to appear and the sun shone with less intensity.

First human presence

Obviously, in order to find human features in the region we must make a giant leap forward, to approximately the year 1200 BC, when it is thought that the Anasazi arrived. These were the first ancestors of the Pueblo Peoples, an indigenous American tribe who used to live in the shelter of the cliffs, building stone and adobe clay dwellings. Other ancient populations of the Grand Canyon include the Cohonina, who lived on the banks of the western shore between the years 500 and 1200, and who were the ancestors of the Yuma, the Havasupai and the Hualapai, who today share the land with the Pueblo Peoples.

Europeans did not settle in the region until the 19th century, three centuries after López de Cárdenas's discovery. After several decades of trying, in 1869, New York biologist, geologist and soldier John Wesley Powell organised the first expedition capable of crossing the 446 km (277 mi) from one side of the Grand Canyon to the other, taking with him nine men, four boats and provisions for ten months' travel. After achieving this, Powell drew upon his scientific streak to confirm that the strata of layered sedimentary rock on the walls of the narrow pass 'were like the pages

↑Mather Point Another of the views of the Grand Canyon, from the extreme south.

↗Skywalk This 1,200 m (3,937 ft) high platform, offers some exceptional views.

↗Californian condor This is one of the most characteristic and protected species of the national park.

→Colorado River For centuries, the riverbed has been sculpting the walls of the Grand Canyon.

↑Vegetation The Grand Canyon has more than 1,500 plant species.

of a large history book'. In fact, it was Powell who named this geological marvel, which he had just dared to go through, the Grand Canyon. In 1903, President Theodore Roosevelt, a great nature lover, visited the narrow pass and decided to establish a hunting reserve, despite opposition from landowners and mine owners in the region. For this reason, it was not until 1919 that the Grand Canyon National Park was created. This protected region receives more than 4.5 million visitors every year and has a diversity of ecosystems due to the significant variations in altitude and exposure to the sun. The vegetation is characterised by the Sonora Desert, an arid ecosystem which extends over the surface of both sides of the border between the United States and Mexico. Among the fauna, there is the Californian condor, one of the most majestic birds on Earth, the peregrine falcon, the grasslands rattlesnake, the puma, the lynx, the coyote and the Rocky Mountain goat, once a very common species in the region but today very difficult to spot, largely due to it being hunted during the 19th century.

History of the Earth

The 1,500 m (4,921 ft) deep Grand Canyon constitutes a geological testament of incalculable value.

Californian condor *(Gymnogyps californianus)* After becoming almost extinct at the end of the last century the Grand Canyon was repopulated with condors raised in captivity.

Clear layers These layers are formed from Coconino sandstone and sea sediments (Toroweap), and have traces of vertebrates.

Red layers The three primary layers are Temple Butte and Redwall, both limestone rocks which contain a large number of fossils, and the Supai group of red sandstones.

Greyish layers The Tonto group, formed 500 million years ago, has various horizontal layers with sandstone and limestone shale.

Dark layers In the deepest layers, which continue to be eroded by the Colorado River, there are rocks approaching two thousand million years old. When they were created, they were subject to very high temperatures.

Coyote *(Canis latrans)* Lives close to the banks of the river, but it is difficult to see. It is more common to hear it howling.

Flora and fauna The Grand Canyon National Park has one of the richest ecosystems in the United States. It has all types of forest and desert, in addition to some 350 species of birds, and another 150 of mammals, reptiles, amphibians and fish.

An incredible view The Skywalk, built in 2007 with the approval of the Hualapai tribe, is a large circular platform with a glass floor which projects 20 m (66 ft) outwards and offers spectacular views of the Grand Canyon.

TONGARIRO

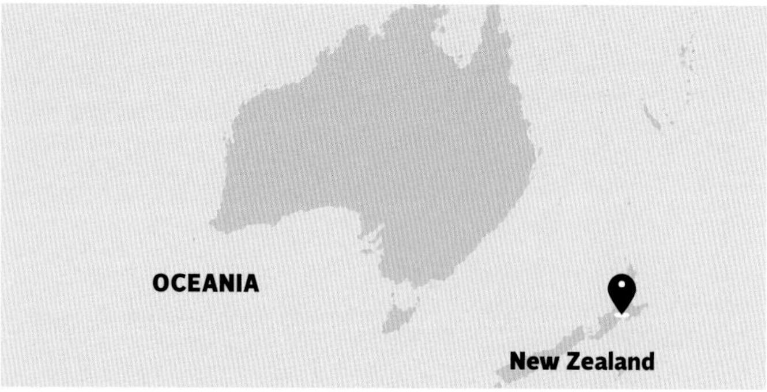

Tongariro This National Park, declared a World Heritage Site by UNESCO, is located in the centre of the North Island of New Zealand and covers an area of 796 km^2 (307 mi^2).

The beauty of volcanoes

In New Zealand's North Island, the Pacific Ring of Fire reveals its most spectacular side with active volcanic landscapes that delight hikers.

Divided into two large islands, New Zealand has one of the most diverse and exciting natural landscapes on the planet. The North Island is characterised by its great volcanic activity, while the South Island is an ideal destination for mountaineers and hikers who come from all around the world to see the coasts cut by deep fjords, surrounded by the scenic summits of the Southern Alps. In addition, its population, with a density of just 15 inhabitants per square kilometre, feels tremendously proud of this heritage, and is educated in an integrated way from childhood about how to respect and enjoy nature. Even the larger cities, Auckland, Wellington and Christchurch, appear to have been designed to take advantage of the superb and accessible environment.

With such a positive attitude towards nature, it is not surprising that in 1887, the volcanic region of Tongariro became one of the first national parks in the world. Located in the middle of the North Island, it includes a region occupied by three active volcanoes: Ruapehu, to the south – standing at 2,797 m (9,177 ft) high, it is the tallest on the island; Ngauruhoe rising 2,291 m (7,516 ft), in the centre, and Tongariro, 1,978 m (6,490 ft), in the north, which lends its name to the protected area and which, in fact, forms just one stratovolcano complex of andesite, the most common volcanic rock found on Earth after basalt, and which is also found on the surface of Mars. A few miles to the north of the park is Lake Taupo, the largest lake in the country. It was formed by an enormous volcanic crater the eruption of which, in the year 181, is considered by geologists to be one of the most violent in the last 5,000 years.

A constantly active volcanic region

Mount Tongariro began its eruptive activity around 275,000 years ago. Since then it has remained active, although intermittently, until the most recent explosion: a hydrothermal eruption in 2012. Ngauruhoe has been the most active volcano in recent times, with more than 70 eruptions in the last 200 years. And Ruapehu, the most powerful of the three, began its

↑Under the snow Aerial view of the Tongariro National Park with craters completely covered in snow.

volcanic activity 250,000 years ago and has recently produced some spectacular eruptions every 50 years: 1895, 1945 and 1995. In the quiet periods, its main crater fills with water as a result of the snow that falls in winter which then melts. This combination, together with the occasional expulsion of magma material, converts the water into a warm liquid acid. The last large eruption completely emptied this lake, generating dangerous lahars: avalanches of molten mud that descend the slopes of the mountain at high speed. Despite all these risks, the two largest ski resorts in New Zealand are found on the slopes of Mount Ruapehu, and are very popular with islanders between the months of June and October. Like the rest of the summits in the country, the volcanic section that makes up the park is sacred land for the Māori, the first inhabitants of the islands. In fact, the protected region was created at the request of the influential chief of a local clan with the aim of preventing white settlers from acquiring and exploiting the region. However, the Māori could not avoid the introduction of heather, a phanerogam or flowering plant, covering much of Europe, America and North Africa, which was brought to the region a century ago and planted to prepare for another invasive species, the wood grouse, which was released to encourage hunting in the park. Although the project was never finished, this curious and antiquated idea in a protected area caused serious damage, as the heather has spread over the territory, putting the equilibrium of the ecosystem and the existence of various native species of plant at risk.

The presence of three active volcanoes within the park's boundaries might suggest that the area's vegetation is rather poor. However, the northern and western parts of the protected region are home to wide swathes

↑Ruapehu Spectacular view of the snow-capped mountain from the city of Ohakune.

↗Emerald Lakes Around the skirts of Tongariro are three beautiful lakes. Their colour is caused by dissolved minerals.

→Red Crater An obligatory site for the tourists visiting Mount Tongariro.

↑Kiwi This is the official mascot of New Zealand. The roads are lined with signs warning drivers about the danger vehicles pose to kiwis.

of subtropical forest of native conifers with abundant orchids and ferns which provide an almost jungle-like environment. In some mountain regions, located 1,500 m (4,921 ft) above sea level, there are beech trees covering the sparse upper plains which have not been affected by the volcanic badlands: fields of gravel between which grow buttercups and other types of vegetation capable of resisting the aridity of the land and the cold climate of the summits.

The ecosystem is inhabited by some interesting native species, such as the popular kiwi, which shares the land with animals introduced from Europe, including deer, weasels, rabbits, hares and possums. The kiwi is a flightless bird which has become one of the symbols of New Zealand to the point that New Zealanders are known around the world as kiwis. Another of the country's symbols, this one much more recent, is the film trilogy *Lord of the Rings*, much of the filming for which took place on the steep volcanic slopes of this wonderful park.

Trekking paradise

The National Park of Tongariro is a tourist destination that is much loved for its impressive hiking trails.

A highly active volcano Tongariro has recently registered a significant amount of activity. In August and November 2012, its latest eruptions occurred in the uppermost vent, Te Maari, on the north face of the volcano.

North crater When it was created, molten lava filled the crater and then cooled and solidified to form a flat surface 1 km (0.6 mi) across.

Mount Tongariro (1,978 m / 6,490 ft)

Mount Ngauruhoe (2,291 m / 7,516 ft) This is the youngest vent of the volcanic group and one of the most active.

Southern crater

Tongariro alpine crossing This is one of the most famous hiking routes in the world. It covers 19 km (11 mi) and covers the entire volcanic region between the mountains of Tongariro and Ngauruhoe.

Lake Taupo Located next to the Tongariro National Park, it is the largest lake in New Zealand and covers a surface area of 606 km² (234 mi²). This stretch of water is fed by the Waikato River through the crater of an old volcano which in the year 181 caused the largest eruption recorded on Earth in the last 5,000 years.

Sacred place The Māori decorated some of the rocks around the lake with faces and other images.

Mount Ruapehu (2,797 m / 9,177 ft) In addition to the main peak (Tahurangi), it has two secondary peaks measuring 2,755 m (9,039 ft) and 2,751 m (9,026 ft). In winter its sides become the largest ski slopes on the island.

Emerald lakes At the base of Tongariro, these three lakes of greenish waters and yellowish shores, caused by sulphur, are one of the most beautiful places in the National Park.

Large rock Alongside Tama Superior, at the foot of Mount Ngauruhoe, there is an enormous volcanic rock which is a must-see for hikers.

Based on an idea by Joan Ricart
Editorial coordination Marta de la Serna
Design Clara Miralles
Editing Alberto Hernández
Copy (supplied by) Ricard Regàs
Graphic editing Alberto Hernández
Translated by Sol90 S.L.
Layout Paola Fornasaro, Clara Miralles
Copy Editor Stuart Franklin
Infographics Sol90Images
Photography AGE Fotostock, Getty Images, Thinkstock, Cubo Images, Corbis, Istockphoto